STRATHCLYDE

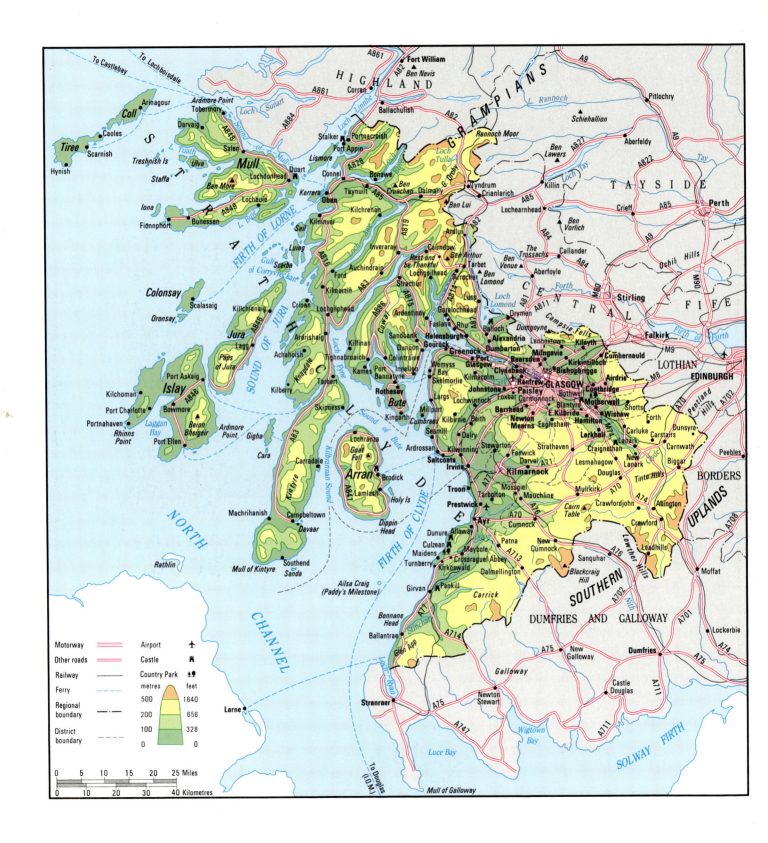

To Castlebay   To Lochboisdale

HIGHLAND

A861   Fort William
Ben Nevis
Corran
A82
A861   Ballachulish
A82
Loch Sunart
A884
Ardmore Point
Tobermory
Arinagour
Coll
Caoles
Tiree
Scarnish
Hynish

Darvaig
Salen
A848
Ulva
Mull
Ben More
Iona
Lochbuie
Fionnphort   Bunessan
Treshnish Is
Staffa

Lismore
Loch Linnhe
Stalker
Portnacroish
Port Appin
A828
Duart   Connel   Bonawe
Kerrera   Taynuilt
Oban   Ben Cruachan
Kilchrenan
Kilninver
Seil   Loch Awe
Luing
Scarba
Gulf of Corryvreckan

Colonsay
Scalasaig
Oronsay

Kilchianaig
Jura
A846
Lagg
Paps of Jura
Craignish   Crinan
Lochgilphead
A816
Ford   A83
Kilmartin
Ardrishaig
Achahoish
Knapdale
Tarbert
Kilberry

Islay
Port Askaig
A846
Kilchoman
Port Charlotte
Bowmore
Portnahaven   Beinn
Rhinns   Bheigeir
Point   Port Ellen
Laggan Bay

Gigha
Ardmore Point
Cara

Kintyre
A83
Carradale

Machrihanish
Campbeltown
Davaar
Southend   Sanda
Mull of Kintyre

Rathlin

Larne

SOUTH

FIRTH OF LORNE
SOUND OF JURA
SOUND OF MULL

Tuath
Sound of Mull

GRAMPIANS

A9
Pitlochry
L. Rannoch
Schiehallion
Rannoch Moor
Loch Tulla
L. of Orchy
Aberfeldy
Ben Lawers
A827
Tyndrum   A82   Killin
Crianlarich   A85
Lochearnhead
Ben Lui   A85
Crieff
A85   Perth
Ardlui   A82
Loch Tay
A822

TAYSIDE

Cairndow
A83   Ben Arthur
Rest and   Tarbet
be Thankful   Ben Lomond
Lochgoilhead   Arrochar
Strachur   Luss
A815   A814   Loch Lomond
Ardentinny   Garelochhead
Colintraive   Balloch
Kilfinan   Rhu
Tighnabruaich   Faslane
Kames   Sandbank   Helensburgh
Port   Dunoon   Gourock
Bannatyne   Port   Greenock
Rothesay   Glasgow   Port
Bute   Wemyss   Glasgow
Bay   Kilcreggan
Skelmorlie
Largs
Millport
Cumbraes   Lochwinnoch
Seamill   Kilbirnie
Dalry   Beith
Kingarth
Ardrossan   Kilwinning
Saltcoats   Stewarton
Irvine   Fenwick
Troon   Kilmarnock
Prestwick   Tarbolton   Mauchline
Ayr   Mossgiel
Dunure   Cumnock
Alloway
Culzean   Maybole
Maidens   Crossraguel Abbey
Turnberry   Kirkoswald
Girvan   Penkill
Dalmellington
Carrick
Bennane
Head
Ballantrae
Glen App
A714
A77

CENTRAL

The Trossachs
Callander
A84
Ben Venue
Aberfoyle
Ochil Hills
Forth
A81   A811   Stirling
Drymen
Dumgoyne   Campsie Fells
Lennoxtown
Milngavie   Kilsyth   Falkirk
Bearsden   Kirkintilloch   Cumbernauld
Bishopbriggs   M9
Clydebank   Airdrie   M8
Renfrew   GLASGOW   Coatbridge
Paisley   Bothwell   Motherwell
Johnstone   Blantyre   Wishaw
Barrhead   E. Kilbride   Hamilton   Shotts
Newton   Eaglesham   Larkhall   Forth
Mearns   Strathaven   Carluke
Darvel   Lesmahagow   New Lanark   Carstairs
A71   Douglas   Tinto Hills
Muirkirk   A70   Biggar
Crawfordjohn   A74   Carnwath
New   Cairn   Abington
Cumnock   Table   Crawford
Sanquhar   Leadhills
Blackcraig   Lowther Hills
Hill
Moffat

LOTHIAN
FIFE
BORDERS

M80
M9
A80   M8
Falkirk   Firth of Forth
Stirling   M90
Forth

Pentland Hills
A702
EDINBURGH
Dunsyre
Carstairs
A70   Peebles
Carnwath
A72
Biggar
A721
UPLANDS
A708

SOUTHERN
UPLANDS

DUMFRIES AND GALLOWAY

A76   New
Cumnock
Sanquhar
Blackcraig
Hill
A702
A701
Nith
Moffat
Lockerbie
A74
Dumfries
A75
New   A711
Galloway
Castle   A711
Douglas
A75

Galloway
Stranraer
A75   Newton
Stewart
A747
Wigtown
Bay
Luce Bay
Mull of Galloway
Solway Firth
A711

FIRTH OF CLYDE
Ailsa Craig
(Paddy's Milestone)
Arran
Lochranza
Goat Fell
Brodick
Holy Is
Lamlash
Dippin Head
Sanda
Kilbrannan Sound
Sound of Bute
Carrick

NORTH CHANNEL

To Douglas
(I.O.M.)

Legend

Motorway	Airport ✈
Other roads	Castle ⚔
Railway	Country Park ♦
Ferry	
Regional boundary	
District boundary	

metres	feet
500	1640
200	656
100	328
0	0

Scale:
0 5 10 15 20 25 Miles
0 10 20 30 40 Kilometres

STRATHCLYDE

PHOTOGRAPHED BY DOUGLAS CORRANCE
WITH COMMENTARY BY EDWARD BOYD

COLLINS

Glasgow and London
in collaboration with Strathclyde Regional Council

The Publishers wish to thank Paul Gunnion for his
additional captions, and the Scottish Tourist Board
for permission to reproduce the photographs
by Douglas Corrance on the following pages:
8, 9 (top), 10 (bottom), 11-15, 18, 19, 26-29, 31-37,
38 (right), 39-45, 48 (top left), 50 (bottom), 57-73,
74 (top right and left, bottom left), 75-77, 78 (top right
and bottom left), 79, 84 (top left), 89 (bottom left and
right), 90, 91, 94, 96, 97 (top right and bottom left),
105, 107 (top left), 110-112, 113 (top left and right),
115 (top right, bottom left and right), 119, 120 (top).

Published by William Collins Sons and Company Limited
First published 1985
© William Collins Sons and Company Limited

Cartography by Mike Shand
Typeset by John Swain and Son Ltd, Glasgow
Colour reproduction by Arneg Ltd, Glasgow
Printed in Great Britain by Collins Glasgow

ISBN 0 00 435691 8

INTRODUCTION

Sir Oswald Sitwell once said that he was educated during the holidays from Eton, and when I read that statement I knew immediately what he meant. Not that my schooldays ever took me anywhere near Eton and, indeed, I am not even certain to this day where the place is, my own experience of public schools being confined to the creations of Frank Richards. I have never on this account regarded myself as being, in any way, deprived. What I may have lost on the swings of Eton I gained from the roundabouts of the fictitious Greyfriars, and if I was never privileged to have some future minor politician fagging for me, I had the possibly preferable company of Billy Bunter and his persecutors in *The Magnet* every week.

My grandfather used to say that he was educated at the tail of a cart, a claim that fascinated me as a child until I was able to recognize it for the metaphor it was. Long after my grandfather was dead I learned a piece of family folklore to the effect that, as a boy, he carried a book wherever he went, at the insistence of the uncle who brought him up. Thus, jolting along Irish country lanes, he learned from whatever books came his way, and a rum lot they were, ranging from *East Lynne* to Plato. What he made of *The Republic* I do not know, although I would hazard a guess that, as a staunch Orangeman, he was probably agin it. I do recall, though, that he always referred to Socrates as Soccerahtees, and when I watched the brilliant Brazilian footballer of the same name when the World Cup was televised, I had the weirdest feeling of *déjà vu*, as though I was watching someone whom my grandfather had invented.

What I am saying here is that, in a strange way, Sir Osbert Sitwell and my grandfather were, basically, saying the same thing. In essence, they were stating a fundamental belief in education as something worthwhile, and at the same time they were cocking a snook at those institutions that reduce it to a commodity by claiming a monopoly of it. To those who may think that I am reading too much into Sir Oswald Sitwell's remark, I can only say that if Sir Osbert had really decided that education was a write-off, he had plenty of other options available for passing the time. As an aristocrat he could have slaughtered birds and animals, or he could have become one of the unspeakable in pursuit of the uneatable. At some point a choice had to be made and a balance struck between the cerebral and the physical, and perhaps education can be defined as the making of that choice.

It is not enough, of course, simply to make the choice. My grandfather did, but much good it brought him. He died a very frustrated little man and a man whom I remember as always seeming vaguely puzzled, as though he had been vouchsafed a glimpse of something marvellous and deeply important and had then forgotten it. Perhaps it is always easier for the Sitwells of this world. They know the right people and the right avenues of access to what they want. Between my grandfather and whatever dream he may have cherished there always seemed to be insurmountable obstacles; and the morose drinking of his latter days may be seen ironically as the cup of hemlock that was forced on Socrates.

Of course things are different now, you say, and you may even believe it. All I can say in reply is that such has not been my experience and that all my observation contradicts your assertion. I do not intend to mount any hobbyhorses for the time being since I am still saddle-sore from a previous one. For the moment I shall content myself with saying that I treasure that image of a small boy reading a book on the back of a cart.

When I first got down to doing my part of this book, I found that my education, as it had proved to be on so many previous occasions, was of no help to me at all. Certainly I had heard of Strathclyde and had indeed lived there for a great part of my life. Yet my knowledge of the place was, at best, wispy and, at worst, thoroughly jumbled. My memory recalled it as the geographical equivalent of a movable feast that sometimes was confined to Dumbarton and its outskirts and sometimes aggrandized itself as far down as Cumbria. There was a king too who got confused in my mind with Telly Savalas but who is known to history as Owen the Bald. Not a great deal, I said to myself; a poor return for all those boring, imprisoned years in classrooms, listening to the drone of so-called teachers as they gradground the fascination of history into a dust as grey as themselves. Then it gradually dawned on me that I was missing the point, which was that the concept of Strathclyde had managed to survive during all these hundreds of years. I suddenly saw Strathclyde as a kind of psychological government in exile, awaiting with a grim, unnoticed patience its moment of recall. That moment came with the Wheatley Report on the re-organization of local government, and in May 1975 Strathclyde Region emerged triumphantly from the mists of exile.

As I strove to put words to Douglas Corrance's brilliant photographs, I began to feel increasingly that I was dealing with a country rather than a region. There were various reasons for this feeling, many of which, no doubt, can be inferred from my captions. One reason, however, that cannot be inferred from them but which must be brought to notice is the fact that Strathclyde Region contains half of the population of Scotland. This, I submit, has a great bearing on how Strathclyde is viewed by the rest of the country. Their attitude always seems to conceal a fundamental unease, an unease that is a kind of tacit admission that they, too, have a sneaking suspicion that Strathclyde may be something more than a region, an unease that is always present when a small country is contiguous to a larger or more powerful neighbour. In a different context, Scotland displays the same unease as far as England is concerned, and Canada evinces it towards the United States.

Staunch Marxists would probably see this fear as economically determined, yet in the case of Strathclyde versus the rest of Scotland we see another factor that people tend to ignore. That is the racial factor. It is possible that with the emergence of Strathclyde we see one of the ironies in which history apparently delights. The great Irish famine sent thousands of Irishmen to settle permanently in the west and southwest of Scotland, while the Clearances drove the Scottish Highlanders south, away from their starvation. This Celtic influx made this particular area of the country what it is, racially and ideologically. Perhaps what the rest of Scotland (and a great deal of England) fears is that with the rebirth of Strathclyde there is also born the potential for a Celtic Republic. Stranger things have happened, and with the access to power of a prime minister who seems to be obdurately convinced that a country can be run by using the same primitive economics that used to govern what we called a Jenny A'Thing shop, we may yet live to tell our children that we saw the last Secretary of State for Scotland; that is, of course, those of us who are lucky enough to live in the Region of Strathclyde.

Edward Boyd

Argyll extends over some 1,990,472 acres, give or take a rod, pole, or perch, and some historians see it as the place where Scotland had its beginnings. The year usually given for the arrival of the Scots is 258, when Cairbre Riada arrived from Ireland with his companions, driven to emigrate by famine, a grim precedent for later. They christened their new home Dalriada, after the place they had left, which was not particularly original of them, but we should not expect too much from starving men. There was a further incursion from Ireland in 498, when the three sons of Erc decided to drop in on their Scottish relatives. The three turned out to be well-doing lads. Fergus was soon the boss of Kintyre, Knapdale, Cowal and Mid-Argyll. Loarn took possession of territory to the north of Mid-Argyll, while Angus, perhaps deciding that the future was in malt whisky, settled in Islay. And thus the Scots were launched into history, and the Picts began their long slow decline into oblivion, where they liked it so much that they have stayed there, resisting all the most determined efforts of researchers and historians.

Argyll, on the map, is like a dictionary illustration to the word 'sprawl'. It seems to have no consistency, and this is part of its charm. The sea around it appears to delight in making sudden and deep thrusts into the land, while the land itself has regular fits of boredom with the level and hurls itself skyward as a mountain. Yet it is capable of a kind of well-mannered docility such as we see in the top picture, taken near Strone, and, to a certain extent, in the picture below which looks across to Davaar Island at the entrance to Campbeltown Loch. The name Davaar is the Gaelic way of saying 'two heights', the kind of statement that scores high on observation but disappointingly low on imagination. We feel that the Pictish name for it would have translated as something poetic like 'green whale'.

It was the kind of day you sometimes get in late spring or early summer, that seems to have come fresh from the laundry. Campbeltown was looking its best: trim, clean and 'bien', to use a Lowland word. Ahead, a clock tower gleamed, reminding us of the dentifrice adverts of long ago, a dentifrice advert with portholes. How had it stayed so clean after centuries of coal mining? Maybe the books were wrong and had mixed Campbeltown up with somewhere else. Even this momentary doubt is itself a tribute to the town's remarkable capacity for survival, its ability never to have all its eggs in one basket. Coal, fishing, whisky, even whaling, Campbeltown has at various times taken them all in its stride. But with the great days of the distilleries and the boats gone and the biggest fish around being Paul Macartney, the town is turning more and more to the tourist industry.

Scots have been chary of the tourist trade, perhaps unduly so. Over the years a peculiarly Scottish attitude has evolved, that says in effect: 'When you've sold everything else, you sell yourself. That's tourism.' This attitude is now being recognized for what it really is — a disguised xenophobia. It represents a kind of undeclared war which, in a world that has become, in McLuhan's phrase, 'a global village', is not only pointless but ludicrous. But there is growing evidence of an unexpected feedback from tourism. We are becoming more introspective in a positive way. Once we asked ourselves why anyone in their sane senses should spend money to come and see us. Now we accept that such people are in their sane senses and that, therefore, we might just have something they consider worth seeing and worth spending money to see. It is a small step but an important one nonetheless. The lady who runs the Campbeltown bookshop has realized this. She has a son in publishing and so is not overawed by publishers. Anything local or with a local connection is, in her view, as worthy of promotion as anything backed by the heavy publicity machines of London or New York. Didn't 'Mull of Kintyre' emerge victorious from the cut-throat world of pop music at number one in the charts? Nor has 'Campbeltown Loch' done too badly. And even 'The Auld Maid in a Garret' could be in with a shout in a world that has shown itself susceptible to celluloid kailyard. This new pride can obviously be transmitted to inanimate objects. The name of the clipper-bowed boat with the Campbeltown registration is perhaps less a name than a claim.

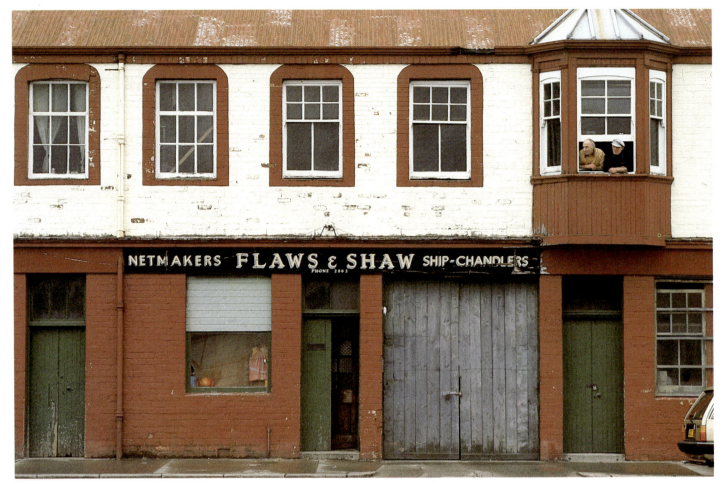

The immediate impression is that they do not really exist; that Dickens invented them in the course of a fleeting and hitherto unrecorded visit to Campbeltown. But they exist all right, though which is Flaws and which is Shaw we are far from certain. We suspect they take it in turns. What is beyond doubt is that for years they have been conducting an argument on the subject of CN253. Is it or is it not a fishing boat? Flaws says the wheelhouse turns what was a vessel into a vehicle. Shaw finds this nonsense and points out that the fish will still be caught by net, not just run over. Flaws wonders sarcastically how many crans CN253 gets to the gallon. Shaw calls him a Luddite, and Flaws departs in a huff to the library. Shaw drifts along to the pub where the skipper of CN253 is engaged in a heated argument about the best place to hang L-plates.

Our initial reaction on seeing the shop in Carradale was to exclaim: 'A Jenny A'thing. Quick! Slap a preservation order on it!' This, of course, is a kind of sentimentality against which we have to be on our guard, for it makes us terrorists in time, demanding to be flown back to the simplicities of yesterday. A Jenny A'thing was a little shop that sold everything you could possibly need. Our Jenny was a Joe, and his shop was in no way as hygienic as this one. It smelt of paraffin and chopped wood and Joe's last meal. He was a freethinker and anarchist who hated the human race with an intensity worthy of a better cause. Not unnaturally, the human race hated him right back, and there was no general mourning when he was found dead one day, ironically slumped over Kropotkin's *Mutual Aid.* He left a surprising amount of money, and we remember this when we get sentimental. Every small store is an embryonic big store, and inside every Joe or Jenny is a Woolworth fighting to get out.

Cassandra, we are told, was a very upper-crust lady. The gods endowed her with the gift of prophecy, but wrote into the small print that she would never be believed. How wise the gods were becomes more obvious by the minute, now that the media have taken over her role without the compulsory scepticism.

People are becoming concerned about the world their children are being offered, yet are doing nothing really positive about it. So many experts have taken over so many aspects of our lives that we accept our powerlessness. Psychologists have even invented for it the term 'learned helplessness'. The time has come to unlearn this helplessness if we are to offer a future to the kids at the Carradale store. Perhaps we could start with a law against the wearing of long trousers by anyone under twelve. This would re-establish a useful *rite de passage* and lead to our eventual goal: the abolition of that artificial and totally economic concept, the Teenager.

Scotland is filled with Tarberts. There is one on Harris, one on Loch Lomond, which spells itself Tarbet, there is what is usually referred to as Tarbert, Loch Fyne, pronounced as one word, and no less than five in Mull, according to James B. Johnston whose *Place-names of Scotland* is a useful emetic for those who see the Gael as living in a perpetual, poetic Celtic twilight. When the Gael baptised, he baptised with total pragmatism, and many of his names were more concerned with straightforward information than the circuitousness of poetry. This is not to deny poetry to the Gaelic mind, which would be a nonsense. It is to suggest that the Gael held poetry in such high esteem that he refused to throw it away on rocks and rivers. The Gaelic *tairbeart* means isthmus but a special kind, one a boat could be dragged across. If there is such a thing as a dry-land canal, *tairbeart* is it, and both Magnus Barefoot and Robert the Bruce had their galleys dragged across the isthmus at Tarbert, Loch Fyne. All over the country, people dragged ships overland, but we are not expected to believe that the Vikings gave up their attacks because their crews, remembering all those *tairbearts,* vetoed Scotland as 'a real drag'.

Tarbert, Loch Fyne, was once a prosperous fishing port, and we well remember an entrepreneur who used to push through the streets of our home town a barrow on which was balanced a box of herring. He had a stentorian voice, and his call of 'Loch Fyne herring' would have wakened the dead. Sometimes he was accompanied by his son, whose heart was in the right place although his brain was somewhere else, for on wet days he carried an umbrella which he held *over the herring.* It would be dramatically neat to have the father grow rich and the son marry a mermaid. Unfortunately, nothing like that ever happened. The strange duo simply vanished, like the herring from Loch Fyne.

Dusk falls on Tarbert Loch Fyne, white buildings scattered along the front like sugar lumps. Lights begin to do their Narcissus bit; everything fades to the hue of a dark grape. Odd how the Reverend James Brown Johnston can reject out of hand the suggestion that the name of the loch comes from a Gaelic word meaning 'vine'. This could be ideological rather than philological. After all, he was minister of Falkirk Free Church for forty years. The boy wonders what it must be like to be a Wee Free for forty years. The girl wonders what it must be like to be *anything* for forty years. Then she wonders what the boy's favourite group is, only to recall that it's Orchestral Manoeuvres in the Dark. She decides to go home while it is still light.

Daylight on the sea wall, and the ambience is astrological. The Twins prepare for an encounter with the Crab or one of his bigger relatives.

It might be said that the first thrust of empire came in 1837, when the young Victoria came to the throne and ushered in the Victorian Age with its splendours and its miseries. It was the age of Dickens and Tennyson, of George Eliot and Mrs Gaskell, of Florence Nightingale and Lord Shaftesbury, of the Pre-Raphaelites and Oscar Wilde. It was the age against which soldiers and sailors, engineers, chemists and clergymen strutted as before a backcloth. It saw a tremendous efflorescence of talent in practically every field of human activity. Yet importantly it was the age of the canal and the railway that killed the canal; and that means that effectively it was the Age of the Unknown Navvy.

To be a navvy, or navigator which was a navvy's Sunday name, was to be doomed to projects that were labour intensive. Employers did not find this daunting or inhibiting, for the Age of Empire was also the Age of the Great Hunger in Ireland, of the Clearances in Scotland. Empty bellies make a full labour market, and these men were shamefully exploited by the employers and vilified and despised by everyone else. One would think that this would lead to feelings of solidarity among the navvies, but apparently the opposite was the case. The despised and rejected fought enthusiastically among themselves until some contractors tried to keep the Scots and Irish segregated on different parts of the job.

It was men like this who built the Crinan Canal, although now only the name of the designer, John Rennie, is remembered. The summit of the canal is sixty-four feet above sea level, and it has fifteen locks, if you are interested in things like that. It runs some nine miles, from Ardrishaig on Loch Fyne to Crinan on the Sound of Jura. It will save you a voyage of 130 miles round the Mull of Kintrye, and you can use the time saved to photograph the natives.

Set out as if for a scaled-up chess game, Kilmorich churchyard on Loch Fyne brings a sigh of relief, and perhaps something more permanent, to travellers from the Rest and be Thankful through Glen Croe.

Below is the Post Office at Bellanoch, on the west side of Crinan Canal. James Hogg wrote a petulant letter from here in 1804, but Mrs McLellan was unperturbed. After all, he was almost a Sassenach, coming from Ettrick, and anyway it was before her time.

We have long been intrigued by the use of corrugated iron as a building material in Scotland. We have come across it all over the country. We even lived in one of those tin houses for a spell and found it very comfortable. An incredible electric storm happened during our tenure there. Giant hailstones dented the roof so badly we had to send for a panel beater.

Jura as seen by the eye of a cruising wild goose. A curiously hostile island in its own quiet way. Not at all like Barrie's Island that likes to be visited, Jura can take you or leave you, so nobody goes there much. The reason vouchsafed for this is lack of accommodation, but we know better, don't we? There are some 'fine raised beaches and caves on the W coast which has never been settled', says one writer, and hurries on as though afraid that someone will ask why that W coast has never been settled. What drew a tubercular Sassenach here to write his work of prophecy? Has anyone noticed the outline, which is that of a pregnant woman? Jura is like Prospero's isle. The air is filled with voices, and always the roar of the whirlpool, Corryvreckan. And, the story goes, if the wind is in the right direction a sad English voice can be heard murmuring 'I was wrong! I was wrong!'.

William of Occam's razor was simply a warning to those wrestling with interpretations of this, that, or the other thing: do not multiply ideas beyond the necessity for them. Take Celtic art, for example. Interpreters have had a field day with its convolutions. Learned theses have been written about serpent worship, giant snakes with their tails in their mouths, representing Eternity. William of Occam would have dismissed such speculation out of hand. What's all this rubbish about giant serpents when the artists were obviously remembering two ropes lying in a boat?

For the benefit of anyone out there who has an ambition to write a sequel to George Orwell's *1984* and who believes that lightning strikes in the same place twice, the following hints may be useful. Jura is an island. This means that if, after a while, you become disillusioned with the project, you cannot just pack it in and walk home.

Jura is twenty-eight miles long and eight miles wide. There is probably a megamillionaire in Dallas who has a car with the same dimensions. The island is not called the Island of the Deer for nothing. If you're allergic to Bambi, stay away.

Stay close to your typewriter and be safe. George Orwell sailed too close to Corryvreckan and nearly ended his career there and then. Whirlpools take no notice of literary reputations. They can't read.

'Colonsay,' said the pilot, and the passenger glanced downward. 'How much do I owe you?' he said. The pilot replied that there would be a bill later. 'I always pay cash,' said the mysterious passenger, handing him a thousand-pound note, 'Sorry I've nothing smaller. Just put me down anywhere here.' The pilot gulped, 'but Colonsay has no landing strip.' The passenger brooded, 'This man in Glasgow,' he said, 'told me that from Colonsay you can walk across the sand to Oronsay, and there is a sanctuary cross embedded in the sand and that a fugitive from Colonsay would be immune from punishment when he reached the cross . . .' 'If he remains on Oronsay for a year and a day,' finished the pilot. 'What's your name?' the passenger asked. 'Jack,' said the pilot, and found himself staring at a huge gun. 'Hi, Jack,' said the mysterious passenger. 'Take me to Spain instead.'

The houses are on Tiree (left) and Coll (right), and we wondered about the brick-and-stone Alice bands round the thatching until we found that in some districts the roof was considered a moveable item. The laird provided the walls, the roof you worried about yourself. Experts have pronounced the old black houses aerodynamically sophisticated, which they had to be to withstand winds of up to 130 miles an hour. The people in these houses never locked their doors. To them, keys and locks were anti-social. A Gaelic saying has it: *cho mosach ris a'ghlais,* 'as mean as the lock'.

We interviewed the Devil at one of his favourite spots, looking across the water towards Bowmore. 'Those ten years were critical for me,' he said 'During that decade I stopped being an over-achiever. Those ten years taught me that there is no good idea, no splendid intention, no worthwhile motive that mankind cannot spoil or corrupt without the slightest assistance from me. Now I leave humanity to its own devices, and that has made me the largest multinational in history.' He picked a gowan, stuck it behind his ear, and vanished.

At the top of the street in Bowmore in Islay stands a building that dates from 1769. It was built by the Campbells of Shawfield who were nothing if not literally minded and who conceived the round church of Kilarrow to prevent the devil from hiding in the corners. Never one to take a thing like that lying down, Old Nick struck back. Taking advantage of the fact that at that time there was no duty payable on whisky produced and consumed locally in Islay, the Devil soon turned every home into a distillery.

The result was predictable. Drunkenness became the island's one and only growth industry, everything else, including farming, practically ceased, and the loudest complaints came from the ministers who discovered, ironically, that they had painted themselves into a corner. No one now mentions this, and you will find no mention anywhere of the compromise that was eventually reached. Now Islay has eight distilleries, including one in Bowmore which claims to be the oldest legal distillery on the island, and which dates back to 1779, ten years after the building of the round church on the hill.

Captain Marryat's three most beautiful things were a rose in full bloom, a ship in full sail, and a pregnant woman. For obvious reasons, two of these are not what might be described as museum material, so the barque has the place to itself, which does not appear to upset the curator. But since he is also a schoolmaster, he probably does not get upset easily. He would probably tell you that at one time Islay had the reputation of producing more sea captains than the place was allowed by the law of averages. He would possibly deny that one was the skipper of a Clyde steamer, who shouted testily from the bridge at a lady latecomer: 'The last man iss aye a wumman'.

More than any other method of getting from one place to another, air travel represents most completely an act of faith. Once you have mumbled a response to the air hostess and squeezed past her into the aircraft, you are no longer your own person. You have surrendered yourself and your will almost totally, to an extent that would have delighted Ignatius Loyola. You have made an affirmation, a one-way commitment. What guarantee do you have that you will arrive where the destination board in the airport promised? What happens if the pilot has other ideas? Years ago, we saw a movie in which the late Buster Keaton played a small part. He was a bus driver who suddenly decided that he was bored to the point of extinction with his daily route and routine, and drove off into the wide blue yonder with all his helpless passengers. Ever since then we scrutinize carefully the pilot of every aircraft we fly in, and if he has the slightest resemblance to Buster Keaton we know that we are doomed to arrive at our destination with our nails bitten down to the wrist. Will he take us where we want to go, or will he be liable to sudden brainstorms or unbridling of the ego? Will we end up in Kuala Lumpur instead of Kintyre, as a friend's luggage did? If it can happen to your luggage, it can happen to you.

Another thing: when you finally get back on terra firma, how do you know you are where you wanted to be? It is at such moments that you realize how insular you are and regret all those further education classes you meant to attend. In the plane you swotted up what you could about Islay, but it all seemed to be about whisky. You half-expected to disembark into a landscape suffused in a golden glow, a landscape seen through a glass lightly and a glass of malt whisky at that. You have a momentary sense of being cheated, just as you had when you looked around in search of your first Islay native. The simple statistical fact has embedded itself in your brain that the Exchequer receives about seven thousand pounds in duty for every man, woman and child in the island. And irrationally, you wanted them all to have eyes like wide, golden coins, and to have names like Laphroaig, and to dwell in houses that had weird candle-snuffers on the chimneys, and were called distilleries.

Tiree High School
Ard-Sgoil Thiriodh

Strathclyde
Regional
Council

Nobody remembers when they first appeared. Some say it was on the north side of the island of Tiree, where there was once a township called *Baile nan Craganach,* the Town of the Clumsy Ones. All the Clumsies had twelve fingers, eleven on the left hand, which resembled a bunch of bananas, while the right hand bore a single finger-shaped thing that recalled the Boy Scout knife that could to everything, including taking stones out of horses' hooves. Over the centuries, this had evolved into a lethal weapon, the Clumsies having stumbled accidentally on to the principle of the laser. For reasons no one yet understands, this turned them into ferocious cannibals, with the result that they ate themselves into extinction, or so it was thought. Now it appeared that somewhere, somehow, a tiny group had survived and was seeking to re-establish their ancient dominance.

Increasingly, their strange pink eggs began turning up until Strathclyde Regional Council could ignore them no longer. Children were instructed to move around in groups of not less than five (some wore magic football jersies and McEnroe wristbands as added protection), and word was sent from the semaphore station built by an uncle of Robert Louis Stevenson: 'RED ALERT. CLUMSIES. COPY TO STEVEN SPIELBERG'. Reports came flooding in, none of them reassuring. Seven of the pink eggs had taken over a fishing boat. The crew's fate was unknown.

An unnatural calm descended on the island, broken only occasionally by the sound of the patrol on their motor bikes. One of them reported ominous news. He had seen one of the pink eggs hatching out. A huge Clumsy had emerged from the shattered shell and had immediately started looting a shop, using the finger on its right hand as a glass cutter. The evacuation of the island has begun. Some of the natives refuse to go. They — and their dogs — will face the future whatever it is. Something round and pink is . . .

In old photographs, the fisher lassies, if they happen to be pictured in their rare leisure moments, are invariably armed with knitting needles with which to fight off that troublemaker who goes around dreaming up mischief for idle hands to do. Nowadays, the needles on Tiree have become a knitting machine and the draughty quayside has become a cosy factory. When we suggested to the young lady that we might be in the market for a quiet, scarlet knitted suit, her only objection was that it would bring out the colour of our eyes.

The crofter on the right was kinder, more polite. His portrait was taken by available light, which was daylight with a little help from a paraffin lamp. The light was, perhaps, the only thing available since he had neither electricity nor plumbed water; nor did he seem to miss them, which should give those people who prattle on about relative poverty furiously to think.

The Scottish Nationalist displays a very special teapot which has been used only once, and that was at his christening party. Perhaps, had there been whisky flowing that day instead of tea, Scotland might have declared UDI by now.

The final sad shot shows an elderly native trying to dissuade his dog from emigrating.

'Low and rolling lands give what no highlands allow. If in these the miraculous surprise of cloud is a perpetual new element of loveliness, it is loveliness itself that unfolds when an interminable land recedes from an illimitable horizon, and, belonging to each and yet remote from either, clouds hang like flowers, or drift like medusae, or gather mysteriously as white bergs in the pale azure of arctic seas.' So said Fiona Macleod, and she should know as she was really a well-heeled Paisley man whom his friends knew as William Sharp. We have often wondered about this piece of literary transvestism. Did Sharp figure that if Mary Ann Evans could get away with calling herself George Eliot, he was obligated to restore some kind of balance by taking the name of an elderly Celtic deb? Or was he a kind of nineteenth-century Boy George without Boy George's complete disregard of convention? Anyway, what he or she said about clouds is true, and this is the evidence. We must confess that the girls digging potatoes worries us as not really belonging to the sequence. Unless, of course, they are called Macleod, when it all becomes an elaborate and esoteric pun.

When we decided to visit Coll, various people told us various things about the island. Some of them told us that it was a kind of poor relation of Tiree, smaller in every way — population, natural resources, etc. Others confined themselves to practical advice (three ferries a week and nothing moves on Sundays). What nobody told us was that as soon as we stepped ashore on Coll we were entering Indian territory. We had seen him on the ferry going over from Tiree, his buttercup-yellow van compelling attention immediately, and everywhere we went after that we seemed to keep bumping into him. Increasingly we had a feeling of *deja vu,* then suddenly our memory began a playback of something that had happened a long time ago. We recalled the TV producer's initial excitement at the idea: 'Great! Great! We pick the kid up straight off the plane from Bangalore or wherever. Then we follow him wherever he's bound for, and keep going back at regular intervals to check on how he's getting on, how he's adjusting to his new environment, and, just as important, how his environment is adjusting to him.' Well, it was a good idea while it lasted, and like many another good idea it died beneath a landslide of memos. And in a different way so too did the producer. Perhaps that Indian on Coll was our young man. If so, he might have become a big media personality. On the other hand — who remembers Sabu?

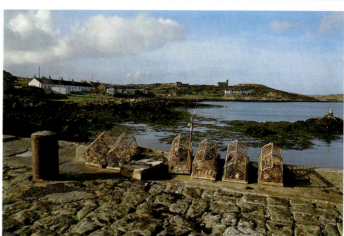

When we read that Coll is two-thirds owned by a Dutch milionaire, our nationalist hackles instinctively rise. Yet it is a pound to a punctured pibroch that a foreign landlord would be hard put to it to compete with the cruelty and insensitivity of the native product. The name of Patrick Sellars is a malodorous one in the Highlands, and that of Colonel Gordon of Cluny deserves to be. Yet it is important not to throw the baby out with the bath water. In 1841 Maclean of Coll decided to clear the island because he reckoned the population was too great and vulnerable. 'He had reportedly impoverished himself buying food for the fifteen hundred people of the island during the recent famine; the motive for the clearance was essentially to diminish the precarious character of life on the island by causing half of the people to leave it and by increasing the amount of land available to the remaining population.' This is from *A History of the Highland Clearances* by Eric Richards, a professor of history in Australia where, ironically, a great number of the displaced ended up. Despite Maclean's social surgery, life on Coll goes on.

The shape, if it can be called that, is one of our earliest memories. It hung on the wall in a terrible lithograph, and for years we thought of it as a cake that had had an unfortunate encounter with the wrong temperature in an oven. This misapprehension was compounded by the vagueness of the printed title beneath the lithograph, which was a victim of fair wear and tear and which seemed to us to read 'Fingal's Cake'. In the fullness of time, of course, we came to know better, but not to feel better, about Staffa and its most famous feature. We preferred it when it was Fingal's Cake, and we still do.

There are certain people and things that seem to be inherently fatal to the Arts. Mary, Queen of Scots is, perhaps, the most celebrated example of this. We have long been convinced that she has proved just as deadly a *femme fatale* to generations of Scottish writers as she was to Riccio, Darnley, and Bothwell. Robert Burns, too, would appear to be a carrier and transmitter of this Writer's Blight. The more that is written about him, the more he remains an enigma. As Staffa remains to us. Once we saw it through childish eyes as a sort of failed cake. Then we saw it as a chunk of rock in the ocean. Now we regard it as the source of some of the worst verse ever perpetrated. Why this should be is baffling. Many of the people who came to visit Fingal's Cave did not lack testimonials. Sir Walter Scott came, and although to us his poetic credentials seem sketchier than most, weighed in with an appalling eighteen lines that can still evoke immediate antiperistaltic action.

Wordsworth's contribution was a short and short-tempered effusion in which he appears to be resenting the presence of his fellow-passengers at what should be his special and peculiar spiritual experience. Sir Robert Peel was as pompous as politicians, apparently,

cannot help being: '[He] had seen the temple not made with hands, had felt the majestic swell of the ocean — the pulsation of the great Atlantic — beating in its inmost sanctuary and swelling a note of praise nobler far than any that ever pealed from human organ.' This is pretty much what you might expect from the man who invented policemen. Others who came were John Keats, J.M.W. Turner, and, inevitably, that lugubrious double act, Victoria and Albert. A constant stream of the famous and the infamous came to goggle at seventy-one acres of volcanic rock.

What did they get from it? What was there that made Felix Mendelssohn want to transpose the experience to music? What brought David Livingstone and Robert Louis Stevenson to add their names to the list of distinguished visitors? Fashion, of course, played a part in it but does not explain the phenomenon which, the photograph suggests, is still viable.

It is almost incredible that Staffa had to wait to be discovered or, more accurately, officially recognized until 1772 when Sir Joseph Banks, on his way to Iceland, was driven by bad weather into the Sound of Mull. His curiosity was aroused by reports of the island with the magical cavern, *An Uamh Binn,* the Cave of Melody. His curiosity led to Staffa and a meeting with the island's solitary inhabitant, a herdsman who lived in a crude hut. We would have liked to have been present at that encounter, when a botanical scientist of the Enlightenment met a herdsman mired in medievalism. Although he did not realize it, Sir Joseph Banks came as the herdsman's executioner. He brought with him new ideas and new values that were to burgeon into the Industrial Revolution, and the cult of Fingal's Cave is a continuing example of bad faith, a futile apology to that herdsman whose way of life was destroyed.

When we think about saints (which, we allow, does not happen too often), we are forced to admit that our attitude towards them is decidedly ambivalent. One side of us is compelled to a reluctant admiration of their courage, steadfastness, and faith, all the qualities, indeed, in which we ourself are singularly lacking. However, co-existing with this is another side which says: name any saint you can think of and you have just named someone we would not want to marry into our family. Take Saint Columba, for example (and wild horses would not make us add that you are welcome to him). He seems to have been a bad loser and a troublemaker, and no doubt there were sighs of relief all round in Ireland when he jumped into his coracle and went off huffily to Iona.

The more we find out about Columba, the less does he come over as your ideal *Guardian* reader.

He was authoritarian, autocratic, sexist, everything that the well-dressed liberal should not be. He could always see both sides of a question, his and the wrong one. He banned cattle from Iona for the following misogynistic reason: 'Where there is a cow there will be a woman; and where there is a woman there will be trouble.' There is a pervading sense of prickliness in Adamnan's seventh-century biography of Columba. Perhaps he felt as we do about saints, but more so since he was in the same line.

One thing about Iona we would like to see cleared up. Several times we have seen the place described in print as a treeless isle. Yet, one writer records Iona as having been famous for its apple orchards. He suggests that an apple a day did not keep the Vikings away in 795 and that the Norsemen slaughtered the orchards with the monks who attended them.

It was an American college that came up with the perfect example of instant history when it decreed: 'From tomorrow onwards it will be a tradition that freshmen do not walk across the lawn.' We see this as the kind of humourless mentality that blights towns before they have even managed to get off the drawing board. Essentially, it is a kind of arrogance based on the doubtful premise that Nanny Knows Best. At its worst it is a fatal denial of organic growth. At its best it can come up with what might be described as a pleasant unreality. We have always regarded Tobermory as a place that was not born but scripted. We were less than surprised, therefore, when someone told us that the multi-coloured houses had been painted that way for the benefit of film cameras. The place has a quality of cinema, which makes the picture on the left of Tobermory Bay almost like a comment, creating a montage of *Mutiny on the Bounty, Drifters,* and an unknown opus called *Sex and the Single Sampan.* The top picture is nature without benefit of cosmetics and shows Ben More, which at 3,169 feet is the highest point of the island. This carries little status, movie-wise, and it looks as though Ben More and the spating burn will have to settle for a place in a calendar advertising some local butcher's prize-winning sausages.

According to ancient superstition, there is special virtue in water that has been used in a baptism. Eyes that have been bathed in it will never see a ghost. This may be why this kind of water never features with Japanese cameras and self-sealing sleeping bags as part of the impedimenta of the conscientious tourist. Such a cleansing would seem to be something to be deplored, for Scotland is the country *par excellence* of ghosts. Duart Castle, in Mull, keeps a renovated eye open for long-gone Vikings; and the three cattle below bring the whole ghost business bang up to date by waiting for nonexistent traffic lights at a ghostly pedestrian crossing.

Last time we crossed in the ferry from Port Appin to Lismore, the man at the wheel was the predecessor of the man in the picture. Or, possibly, the predecessor's predecessor. We spent twenty-eight days on Lismore and for twenty-six of them it rained. Occasionally we took the ferry back to Port Appin on the mainland for the sheer joy of getting soaked in a different ambiance. We are glad to see that the irises (we prefer to call them flags) are still flourishing. They prefer damp places, so Lismore could not happen to a nicer flower.

Lismore lies smack in the middle of Loch Linnhe, and its name, as any Gael will tell you, means 'the big garden'. This is fair enough, for at nine and a half miles long Lismore can hardly be dismissed as a window box. Oddly enough, during our stay we remember best not a plant, not a fruit, but a charming little snail that was whorled in a black and yellow pattern. We remember, too, the old lady who lived next door and was a hundred years old. The West Highland terrier is new, however, and does not meet with our total approval. It could well be one of those anglicized dogs that have never recovered from seeing the lions at the foot of Nelson's column in Trafalgar Square.

Who was Lev Kaleshev and what, if anything, has he to do with Castle Stalker? The answer is nothing, until these three equestrians ride into the picture. The milkiness of the landscape could, perhaps, be another factor in the equation.

Are we going a little too fast for you? Right, first things first. Lev Kaleshev was a Russian and a pioneer film-maker. One day he took a strip of film, a close-up of an actor registering absolutely no emotion at all. He then cut into this film at various intervals various other bits of film, one showing a plate of soup, one a child playing with a teddy bear, a shot of an old lady lying in a coffin. When the film was played back, everyone raved about how marvellous the actor was and how magnificently he had responded to all the stimuli. And that is how film stars were born; or, to put it differently, what real reaction there was came from the viewer's expectation.

If you remove the three riders from the top picture, it is just another view of Castle Stalker, a restored sixteenth-century castle in Appin. The riders, however, bring a rather disturbing new element. Who are they? What are they doing there? It is a curious and rather depressing fact that we never assume good intentions. Left to ourself, we see three quarters of the Four Horsemen of the Apocalypse and immediately start wondering what horrible fate befell the fourth.

In an age of high-rise uniformity, more and more skylines are losing whatever individuality they had. It is easy to understand, therefore, why a building that remains almost defiantly identifiable will engender, even among outsiders, a kind of affection. MacCaig's Tower, in Oban, is like that. When you see it, a precise associativeness says at once what and where it is. With it, Oban is identified as human beings are by fingerprints. Without it, well, Oban would be somewhere else.

There is a shibboleth involved here too. To talk about MacCaig's Folly is to confess yourself a stranger. It is also a depreciation of an act of philanthropy. A sad wisdom advises us that the road to Hell is paved with good intentions. In effect, this is a justification for doing nothing. People who are introduced to the odd circular building as a 'folly' are apt to smile and miss the point, the point being that, far from being a folly in the usual sense of the term (with all its connotations of eccentricity and conceit), MacCaig's Tower was an attempt at a solution to a problem perennially with us — unemployment. John Stewart MacCaig's solution was, on a very reduced scale, what Franklin D. Roosevelt did to haul America out of the Great Depression. Roosevelt could set up an immense programme of public works. MacCaig, operating as a private individual, proposed the building of a museum with a look-out tower rising a hundred feet higher than the walls. In the windows, statues were to be placed, commemorating his family. The project was begun in 1897 and was abandoned after MacCaig died.

There is a story about a Spaniard trying to explain the implications of the word *mañana* to a Gael. The Gael listened politely, then said that in his language there was no equivalent word to denote such a state of urgency. The tattooed lorry on Oban pier suggests that there soon will be.

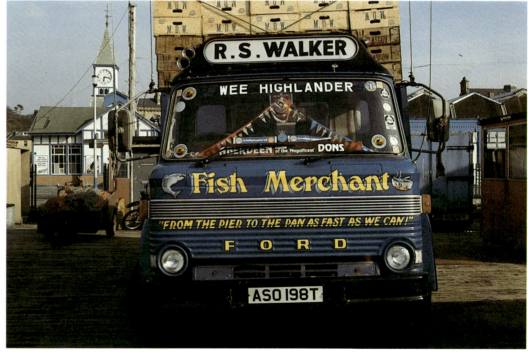

At a seance the other night, we contacted Dorothy Wordsworth via her Japanese guide. 'Where are you speaking from?' she shrieked from the Other World. We told her we were in Oban. 'Ah yes,' she screamed. 'Went there once with William.' There was a long silence, then she said, 'Lovely sunsets there. Fuji, my Japanese guide, y'know, he tells me you've got marvellous things nowadays called cameras.' 'Who would know better than Fuji?' we said, but she wasn't listening. 'Wish William had had a camera on that tour. Might have stopped him spouting those ghastly improvised poems about sunsets and ruined castles and all that rubbish.' 'But I thought . . .' we said, and she sneered. 'You're a Romantic,' she said dismissively. And next day, watching a sailor painting a ship called the *Columba* that no longer goes anywhere near Iona, we realized she was right.

Years ago, when the city we lived in seemed about to change its coat of arms to a simple bulldozer rampant, there was an interesting psychological theory being touted around to account for what seemed to be the arbitrary destructiveness of the city fathers. The theory went something like this: most of the city fathers were men who had come up the hard way. If they pulled down whole districts they were actually trying to wipe out their pasts, painful memories, some recollection of humiliation, some reminder of injury. We never seriously subscribed to this theory, it always having been our experience that people who have come up the hard way are excessively and boringly proud of it. Indeed, in the 1960s a deprived background was a *sine qua non*, and there was a moment when the council house seemed about to topple the castle. The castle fought back, and as we approach the year 2000, the *Jacquerie* would appear to have been put firmly back in its place. The fact that Kilchurn Castle, on Loch Awe, is now a much photographed castle may have something to do with this. The only function of these draughty ruins nowadays is symbolic. They show, in Noel Coward's words, that 'the upper classes have still the upper hand'.

There are signs, though, that the bourgeoisie are catching up in awareness of the importance of having a symbolic architectural past. Industrial archaeology is becoming the in thing. The piece of our industrial past at Bonawe dates back to 1753 when Richard Ford of Lancashire established furnaces and forges for smelting English iron ore. It apparently functioned successfully for a hundred years, which is more than can be said for most of us.

The curtain rises. It is an evening in pre-history. The hills roll away into the distance, practising aerial perspective. They have a strange liquid look, which is not surprising since just a few minutes ago they *were* liquid; they have just heaved themselves into existence and have not yet had time to set properly. A pterodactyl, centre stage, spreads his wings and worries. He is not primarily worried because the hills are still too hot to land on comfortably. What is keeping him awake nights is the uneasy feeling that he might be an anachronism, just an ordinary Joe Pterodactyl trying to get by in an age when pterodactyls are not even on the list of nature's possibilities. He stares over what will eventually be Loch Etive. With a little luck he will wake up tomorrow in the bottom picture, which is twentieth-century Loch Awe with no cormorants.

We are still not certain about where we stand on Unidentified Flying Objects. We read accounts by obviously intelligent men and feel uneasily that there is no smoke without fire. Then we read different accounts which make us feel that they were dreamed up by people who were only a hop, skip and a jump ahead of the men in the white coats with the butterfly nets. Psychologists only tend to confuse us further. One of them says that there is a tendency all over the world to believe in flying saucers and to want them to be real. Anybody in a cinema queue could have told him that, as could anyone who saw something above the thin cloud over Loch Tulla on a wintry day.

The dog in the bottom picture, at Clachan of Seil, has now given up. After ten years he has not managed to make even the local reserve team.

In 1560 the Synod of Argyll ordered the destruction of a stone circle on Iona because it was still in use for pagan worship. These circles, which consisted of a ring of twelve large stones some of which weighed up to a ton, were ancient long before Columba arrived in Iona, indeed, long before the Irish saint was born. One writer states that 900 stone circles are known to exist in Britain and estimates that at least double that number have been destroyed. Our own knowledge of menhirs, a Breton word meaning simply 'long stone', has been garnered from the works of two gentlemen, Goscinny and Uderzo, who are responsible for the continuing saga of Asterix and his inseparable buddy, the menhir delivery man Obelix. Who raised these megaliths and why did they bother? Left to ourself, we would probably have muttered something about Druids and invented an excuse to leave the room. Now it seems that the men in the white nightshirts with the golden sickle and the mistletoe tiaras were latecomers on the scene as far as menhirs were concerned. We shall never put any faith in Goscinny and Uderzo again.

Investigators of the more mystical kind are firmly convinced that these colossal chunks of stone have some strange power. Smiling through our sheer ignorance, we would certainly agree that they have the strong power of creating dissension. The more straight-up-and-down archaeologists deplore a certain kind of theorizing as crude science fiction and attack it as more fiction than science. Those on the wilder shores of theory scream 'Gradgrind' at this attitude and may well be right. At one time the Gradgrinds were scornful of those who saw the megaliths and the way in which they were aligned as astronomical instruments. Now they have been forced to admit to a kind of historical racism and have conceded the possibility that barbarians have brains. This is an important concession. The megaliths here are at Kilmartin and one appears to be foreshadowing the future. The cloud seems to be streaming from its top like an inflammable gas being released from an oil rig.

Walter de la Mare has a most beautiful little poem:

Here lies a most beautiful lady,
Light of heart and voice was she;
I think she was the most beautiful lady
That ever was in the West Countrie.
But beauty vanishes; beauty passes,
However rare — rare it be;
And when I crumble, who will remember
That lovely lady of the West Countrie?

Stone must have seemed an intimation of immortality to primitive men. This is comprehensible when you consider that their life expectation was probably between twenty-five and thirty. Measured against this, stone was for ever. The distorted figures of the soldiers at Kilmartin make one regard the distortion as deliberate, an attempt to accentuate their ferocity and invincibility. Nowadays, we come across this kind of distortion in fashion drawings. Which raises the question: have we progressed or degenerated?

What is so special about the back of a house? Well, to begin with, it's the back of the Auchindrain Farm Museum. Then there are a dozen daffodils (give or take a bloom) for admirers of William Wordsworth. But the real point of the picture is the relevance to the photograph at the top of the opposite page. This is where the running boy is heading. It could hardly be more domestic, more ordinary, less loaded with menace. Yet there must be something inside that surface tranquility that is transmitting the kind of urgent summons that must be obeyed. It has obviously not reached the young lovers yet. Perhaps love is not only blind but deaf as well.

Ever since Sundays found us seated uncomfortably on a hard pew, we have known it; and a multitude of jeremiads have not inclined us to change our mind one tiny bit. There *is* a theatrical tradition in Scotland. The path is there, clear and well defined, but at a certain point along it is a signpost which bears one single ominous word: London. Barrie followed it, with hundreds of others, and look what happened to them. In our opinion, the time has come for the Scottish theatre to mount a sustained attack on received ideas, a Counter Blast against the Monstrous Regiment of Academe. It is time someone took up the cudgels for the Kirk's seminal role in the history of Scottish theatre. Once it was democratic theatre, passionate, prejudiced, political. Modern Scottish theatre, please copy.

Prior to 1939, which was the last year of innocence, the Royal Academy had a charming custom. Its summer exhibition always included a Problem Picture around which the crowds would throng, arguing what the artist was on about. The Press used to get into the act too, and a good time was had by all. It was a naive ritual which did no harm and could only survive in a milieu where the main thrust of art was representational. In these abstract days, when every painting is a problem, the harmless custom has died out, or has it been taken over by photographers? The above picture of Auchindrain Farm Museum is in the tradition; nothing relates to anything else. The lovers inhabit a world of their own. The boy runs round the side of the house, fleeing from what?

The bottom picture shows the curator of the museum modelling an early lawnmower.

Her name was Sarah Murray, and we always see her as a plump little body with dark snapping eyes, her head cocked to one side as she listens, and wherever she is it is raining. We count her with Mungo Park and James Bruce of Abyssinia, although she would have hated them both and, no doubt, the feeling would have been mutual. Her *Companion and Useful Guide to the Beauties of Scotland* is not as well known as similar works by Tennant, Boswell, and John Taylor the Water Poet, but deserves to be, if only for the title.

She was born Sarah Mease in 1744, and at the age of thirty-seven she married Captain William Murray, a naval officer and third son of the Earl of Dunmore. She was widowed at forty, and it was not until twelve years later that she set off on the 2,000-mile tour of Scotland, her account of which begins with invincible practicality: 'Provide yourself with a strong roomy carriage, and have the springs well corded; have also a stop pole and strong chain'.

In her strong, roomy carriage, Sarah Murray traversed Scotland, a true child of the Enlightenment and yet something more. 'The landlord may not at present be hurt in pecuniary matters by the great emigration from the Highlands of Scotland but he and the country at large will ultimately feel its bad effects' is a percipient comment on the Clearances she saw and is perhaps not what we might expect from a work published by an upper-class lady in 1799. Her writing is clear and completely free from the cant and attitudinizing that disfigures so much eighteenth-century writing. Whether she is brooding on the price of potatoes (forty-four pounds for sixpence, the Campbeltown price in 1796) or describing how she executed her scheme to go into the Corryvreckan whirlpool, she remains a lively companion, who said of the place pictured left, 'Inveraray, to me, is the noblest place in Scotland'.

She was eighty-five, and had been off Bute once in her life. That was when she had gone to the north of England as an assistant nanny to some Sassenach lord's children. She stayed three months, then came home for the rest of her days.

We were neighbours in a semi-detached cottage near Rothesay. You would never have known she was there, but she never missed a trick. The postman called her Miss McCallum. She called him Peter in the tone that had known him as a child. Sometimes it seemed she had known everyone as a child.

One ferocious winter night she knocked at our door. When we saw her, we were taken aback, for she kept herself very much to herself. She said, 'I thought you wouldn't want to miss it,' and beyond her, over her shoulder, on the darkness of the Firth of Clyde, we saw the ship. It was the *Queen Elizabeth*, all lit up, moving magnificently, 'Like a floating palace,' she said, making the trite simile sound new-minted. We stood watching in the freezing cold as a spiteful east wind nipped at us. After a while she said, 'I saw the *Titanic* sailing along this way once,' and for a moment the cold felt much, much colder.

The tinkers always came to see her when they were on the island. Years previously she had come across a young tinker woman, lying at the road end, who had gone into labour. Miss McCallum managed with some difficulty to get her into the house, and there her child was born. It was a boy, and, now a hulking man, he used to appear at the back door with a rabbit or a hare or a pheasant. He would do odd jobs for her, then move on.

After we left Rothesay it was some time before we returned. We went back to the house where we had been neighbours, but it was empty and unoccupied. She was probably dead, but we never asked because as long as nobody told us otherwise she was still alive, an old lady who had seen the *Titanic* and was kind to tinkers.

'The castle on the water', the Gaelic name translates, but the castle it refers to is long gone, and the present Dunoon Castle dates back only to 1822. At certain times of the year the place is swarming with people in blue plimsolls and thick white sweaters and funny little woollen bonnets. They are usually accompanied by yachts, which are very prestigious things to have accompanying you. Burns addicts who do not know a spinnaker from a spin dryer will probably be more interested in the farm outside Dunoon where Highland Mary was born. We ourselves once set out to visit this place of pilgrimage but never managed to get there. This was some time ago, and the way of it was this. We had two uncles who were both Burns fanatics and who had decided to add the famous farm to the list of places visited. They never bothered to tell us what they had in mind, so that when we all found ourselves on the Clyde steamer that morning, it was, as far as we were concerned, just an ordinary cruise. In the event, apart from our uncles' intentions, it turned out to be an extraordinary cruise. It was a very calm day, and we remember standing at a rail on the starboard side and thinking how boring water was to stare at when, right before our very eyes, a whale surfaced. There was an immediate rush to the starboard rail, and for a moment or two it seemed as though we were all going to end up on that mighty mammal's back from the canting deck of the steamer. Reason prevailed, or self-preservation, and the steamer was trimmed; and the whale blew a great jet of water skywards, then disappeared under the surface whence it had come. And when we reached Dunoon our uncles vanished into a hostelry to discuss the phenomenon, and somehow Auchnamore Farm and its associations got forgotten. And our uncles went to Canada, and we grew up, for years convinced that Highland Mary was a whale.

Sneer, if you like. Just another piper, you say. Better looking, with a stronger face, than that piper you have on the shortbread tin at home. But did you know that in an inventory of the musical instruments belonging to Henry VIII there appear no less than five sets of bagpipes? Did you know that Perth had a town piper as late as 1831? That the town piper of Dundee was paid twelve pennies a year by every householder in the town? That Geordie Syme, the piper of Dalkeith, was allowed, besides a small wage, a suit of clothes that consisted of a long yellow coat lined with red, red plush breeches, white stockings, and shoes with buckles? That the town piper of Linlithgow was excommunicated in 1707 for immorality? That a court at York decided in the trial of James Reid, a Jacobite of Ogilvie's Regiment, that 'his bagpipe, in the eye of the law, was an instrument of war', and sentenced him to death?

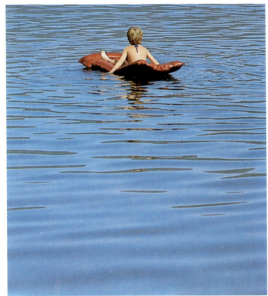

Familiarity with the view of Loch Lomond from the Balloch-Tarbet road seems to contain its scale and grandeur. Our little mariner is quite at home — not a worry in the world. She neither knows nor cares that this is the largest stretch of inland water in Britain, and one of the most beautiful. No mythical monsters, legendary Jacobites, no modern metal projectiles trouble her outlook.

If the ghost of a Jacobite still waits in the gloaming by the pier at Luss for his fellow-prisoner to return by the high road, our little innocent would probably ask the poor wretch if he would like a cup of tea and a cheese sandwich.

Speed boats may sometimes disturb the tranquil waters of Loch Lomond, but only a galley's drag away something faster, silent and more deadly can speed beneath the mirrored surface of Loch Long (right). The navy test-fires torpedoes from Arrochar.

The Jacobite awaiting execution in Carlisle jail would never again walk through Glen Luss with his true love. Recently we have followed in their footsteps in such numbers that the banks and braes are now to be protected from us. We may take the high road as often as we like; we should leave the wilderness unchanged.

This unfamiliar view of Loch Lomond emphasizes our continual need to take a fresh look at all the places which we meekly accept as being beautiful. No need to get your feet wet for a duck's-eye view, as Douglas Corrance has done here, just look again at the familiar and ask yourself: why is this so beautiful?

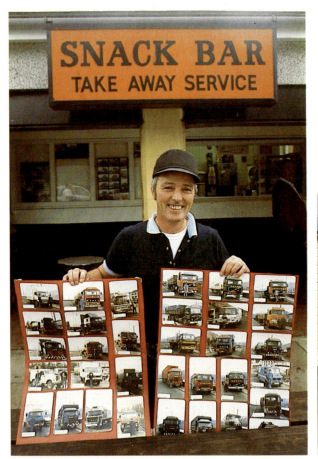

When Suffolks, Shires, Clydesdales, and the occasional Percheron, Brabant, or Boulonnais supplied the motive power for our road-haulage industry, we took them for granted. Now the Albions, Atkinsons and Bedfords, Mercedes, Volvos and Dafs are the driving force in the transport industry and are enjoying their own golden age. All the paraphernalia of nostalgia — books, posters, collections of photographs — proliferate alongside the vehicles themselves, even in Arrochar. We can understand why some haulage firms name their trucks 'Bonnie Lass', 'Wild Rover', 'Prince of Fife', or 'Highland Lad'; horses had such names in their day.

'This must be Arrochar. Shall we have some tea? This looks like a nice place, doesn't it? So welcoming. I think this is just the spot, don't you think so? Perhaps we should spend the night here? I wonder if they have any rooms. Doesn't it look cosy? I really love cosy places. They're so much nicer, aren't they? That little garden is really lovely. Someone has put an awful lot of work into it. That's a good sign, you know. Shows they really care.

'What do you think, dear? Should we stop here and have some tea? We could see what the place is like inside. If it's as nice and friendly as it looks, we could stay the night. What do you think? Shall we do that?'

'Mm. That other place we passed at the pierhead looked all right.'

If traditional songs are an indication of our national state of mind, we have had a soft spot for soldiers and sailors, if not for what they did. Scots have contributed a fair share, perhaps more, to the tales of heroes and villains, lovers and vagabonds, in navy blue, scarlet, and khaki, but their occupation is now so fraught with overtones of universal doom that it is hard to imagine a singer winning a smile or stealing a tear with a sentimental song about Jack Tar and Jenny Wren of Faslane. The singer's sympathies would probably lie with the people of the Peace Camp across the road.

In their pleas for our suppoort, the Peace Camp people have appropriated powerful symbols. Martin Luther King's dream for his people has been extended to all people, wherever and whatever. The green tree of life and the benign sun in the blue sky defy the threat of nuclear winter, but the flowers are ambiguous, for poppies symbolize the sacrifice that friends should never again be called upon to make. The rainbow and the star are ominous. Curving through the sky to burst into white light, this is too much like the doom machine the peace people want us to save ourselves from.

At Rhu, no such horror intrudes on the scene. Weekends of freedom before the breeze ride at anchor, and children gently swing as the sun sets slowly in the west to rise again, and again, and again.

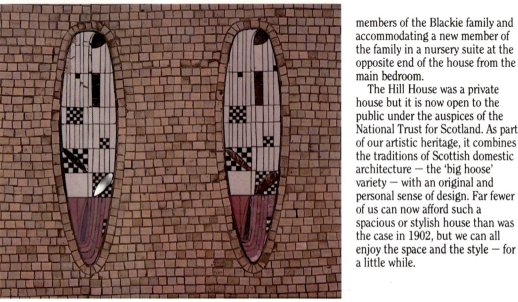

Only the details of the gate to The Hill House in Helensburgh give any hint that this austere-looking house was designed by Charles Rennie Mackintosh for the Scottish publisher, Walter Blackie. The severe approach leads to a spectacular entrance hall which has all the essential characteristics of Mackintosh's style. The series of rectangles, the liking for groups of vertical lines, imply a rigidity which is belied by the decoration on the wall panels in the hallway and by this detail from the mosaic decoration on the fireplace in the main drawing room. Mackintosh's lack of rigidity included designing furniture — ordinary comfortable-looking furniture — for specific members of the Blackie family and accommodating a new member of the family in a nursery suite at the opposite end of the house from the main bedroom.

The Hill House was a private house but it is now open to the public under the auspices of the National Trust for Scotland. As part of our artistic heritage, it combines the traditions of Scottish domestic architecture — the 'big hoose' variety — with an original and personal sense of design. Far fewer of us can now afford such a spacious or stylish house than was the case in 1902, but we can all enjoy the space and the style — for a little while.

ERECTED IN 1872
TO THE MEMORY OF
HENRY BELL
THE FIRST IN GREAT BRITAIN WHO WAS
SUCCESSFUL IN PRACTICALLY APPLYING STEAM
POWER FOR THE PURPOSES OF NAVIGATION

BORN IN THE COUNTY OF LINLITHGOW IN 1766
DIED AT HELENSBURGH IN 1830

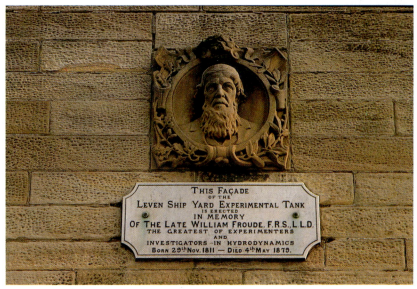

THIS FAÇADE
OF THE
LEVEN SHIP YARD EXPERIMENTAL TANK
IS ERECTED
IN MEMORY
OF THE LATE WILLIAM FROUDE, F.R.S., L.L.D.
THE GREATEST OF EXPERIMENTERS
AND
INVESTIGATORS IN HYDRODYNAMICS
BORN 28th NOV. 1811 — DIED 4th MAY 1879.

Helensburgh, on the north bank of the Clyde, is the nearest resort to
Glasgow, very practically placed for a douce country town. This approach
to life was a characteristic which several of its residents adopted, to the
everlasting benefit of the rest of the world as well as Helensburgh itself.
There is a lovely coincidence about the café proprietor in the birthplace of
the inventor of television seeing and selling the entertainment value of the
first of the broadcast media.

This building in Alexandria would probably have delighted the late Sir John Betjeman. It may look like a Victorian town hall, but in fact it was a factory where, between 1905 and 1914, motorcars were built by the Argyll Motor Company of Scotland — more, the company claimed at one point, than by any other manufacturer in Europe. Legal difficulties in 1914 led to the liquidation of the company, but in the 1920s it returned to Hozier Street in Bridgeton, Glasgow, where Alexander Govan had started to build horseless carriages in 1899, adding one and a half horsepower French engines to a chassis and wheels built from bicycle parts. The Argyll pictured here dates from the company's later Glasgow years, in particular 1927, and has its home now in the city's Transport Museum. Meanwhile, in Alexandria, a splendid Victorian home awaits yet another occupier.

These goose-stepping guards protect the capital, or should it be liquid, assets of a major whisky company in Dumbarton. We have no records, unfortunately, to show that the Romans, who had a Capitol example back home, used geese to guard themselves on Dumbarton Rock, but the protection afforded by the Rock's shape and position made it the capital seat of the kings of Strathclyde, who called it *Alcluith* — the Rock of Clyde. The name Dumbarton is from Gaelic and means 'hill' or 'fort of the Britons'.

Within the Castle on the Rock, we consider that the eighteenth-century Governor's House should not look as tranquil as the gardens at nearby nineteenth-century Balloch Castle, on the shores of Loch Lomond. We feel that Dumbarton Castle should still show some signs of its long and bloody history as fortress, prison, and garrison, not only for the rulers of ancient Strathclyde but for later rulers of Scotland, including Mary, Queen of Scots. It should be bustling with military activity. After all, the Union of the Parliaments, as yet unrepealed, did decree that Dumbarton Castle must always be garrisoned.

Where have you seen that lovely face before, now telling the time in Milngavie town centre? A sharp eye for detail will help, but even better would be a memory of Sauchiehall Street when cars and buses, or even trams, travelled east and west as well as people. A pace more leisurely than our friend's circumnavigation of Mugdock Reservoir would also be an advantage. Cinema fans who remember when the Cosmo and the Savoy and La Scala offered entertainment have the edge as well as those for whom shopping partners did not mean only Marks & Spencer, but also Pettigrew & Stephens, and . . . Copland & Lye.

They know their worth as well as the time in Milngavie. Not for our runner the Glasgow Marathon and all that competition from Bearsden. To be here on Marathon Sunday ensures Glasgow's water supply from Loch Katrine all to himself.

There may be no such thing as a pot of gold at the end of the rainbow, even in Milngavie, but many an investment manager travels into Glasgow every day on the Blue Train in search of it.

Did Lollius Urbicus, back in AD142, ever imagine that the Painted People from whom he was defending the Roman Empire would build their own walls, let alone their own luxury Bearsden barracks? Those who draw a close parallel between Rome and the modern world could argue that Lollius was Manager, North Britain, for Rome Enterprises Inc., a useful posting on the career path between Germany and Africa. *He* built the Antonine Wall to keep the Picts out, but it was named after his boss.

When the grandfathers of the youngsters below played football in Clydebank, they wore tackety boots and boiler suits, the goals were four piles of jackets, mufflers, and caps, and the cranes would have been birling and swinging in the yards as sheets of steel were lowered into place at a time when the Clyde built a third of all the world's ships. It has been said of these yards, and of the others on the Clyde, that they did not just build ships, they built men. It should also be said that this point was made in defence of these Clydebuilt men when they were fighting to save the yards for themselves and their sons and grandsons. In the chilly economic climate of the 1970s and 1980s, with few yards still operating and fitting out oil rigs now, not ships, the lamp standard by the shipyard gate — a wilting flower, its petals shed — can be seen as a symbol of the working life of Clydebank, while in the empty yards daisies, dandelions and rosebay willowherb are flourishing quietly, just as they did before, when the Clyde fell silent between the shipbuilding booms of the two world wars.

Meanwhile, Clydebank improves its appearance by cleaning and renovating its sandstone tenements. The grime and soot of its industrial heyday are scrubbed away, and the interiors refurbished. Someone has made improvements of their own, and in the search for light and a sense of space completely remodelled the window frames. Does renovation include putting right the mistakes of piecemeal improvements?

When the game is finally over and the boots are hung up for the last time, home for our heroes may just as easily be a flat in Clapham, or Coventry, or Cumbernauld, as Clydebank. They are more relaxed and less formal than in any team photographs their grandfathers may have had. There is much more of themselves in their faces: relaxed, happy, nonchalant, or eager. One young man, red and white, front row, extreme right, looks keen enough to bite a few legs. The referee would do well to keep an eye on him, and he should ask the yellow team to find another goalie's jersey, so that we can find the goalie.

The view from Gleniffer Braes over Foxbar and Paisley to Clydebank proves that if you want to take a good long look at the world you live in, you do it best with your feet planted firmly on high ground. Flying out of Glasgow Airport to a holiday on the Costa Plenty or a business meeting in Capital City, you cover the same ground but at such a speed you can gain only a quick impression. Stand here and you can take it in, all of it, in your own time.

In seven thousand years of civilized life, probably only several thousand people have looked across the Clyde valley from Gleniffer Braes. During almost all of that time, a day's journey from here would have taken us as far as Campsie Fells; to Loch Lomondside only if we started early and hurried all the way. Now a day from Glasgow Airport will take us to Jericho, the oldest city in the world, and beyond. One explanation of jet lag says our souls have become so accustomed in seven thousand years to life at a walking pace that they cannot keep up with jets. As a result, we feel ill at ease after a plane journey until, usually the next day, our souls catch up with our bodies. Compared with the thousands who have gazed across at the Campsies and Ben Lomond, millions of people in the past twenty years have seen the Clyde valley from the height of those clouds. Perhaps that is why airports are such soulless places.

GOW 1984

Nowadays, no city can hold up its head in the presence of its peers unless, at least one day a year, it can bring thousands of its citizens out on to the streets, clad in singlets and shorts and prepared to run 26 miles and 385 yards. Despite the name and its associations, the marathon is a modern concept; one pundit even says that the Greeks would have rejected the idea of running 26 miles in one's underwear as the kind of extremism which the best minds of the time had taught them to despise. A gentleman should be able to play the flute, said Aristotle, but not too well. The twentieth century, less inhibited, sees things differently. Doctors, lawyers, and Indian chiefs, labourers and accountants, plumbers and their mates, actors and actresses, taxmen and taxidermists, social workers, social climbers, waiters, every profession listed in Yellow Pages plus some that are not, they all line up south of the Tolbooth as the moment approaches. They would be mildly amused to learn that they outnumber the original

Greek army of 9,000 that fought against and defeated the larger Persian army in 490 BC. They might even think it irrelevant.

They do a little jogging dance as they wait for the off. A sudden autumnal wind nips round their ankles. They remember wistfully that it is Sunday morning and that they should still be snug in bed at this time, with breakfast, the Sunday papers, or the church bells identifying the day. But this day has a different, a special identity, a new addition to the calendar. Palm Sunday, Mothering Sunday, and now Marathon Sunday.

Seconds to go. This is what all the bad jokes and leg pulling have been about. All the discussions of stride patterns and pain thresholds and dehydration. All that pounding of pavements. A great surge, and the Glasgow Marathon, the largest in the world after New York and London, is under way.

Marathon runners are not keen to burn on *the* day, which is perhaps what gives Glasgow its edge, yet the colour of sunshine suits the city which has begun at last to beat its own drum. Now, even the tulips in George Square are harmonized.

Spring marches down an avenue of blossom. In the distance stands the cathedral, a rock in an encroaching pink tide. That Edinburgh grew round a castle and Glasgow a cathedral, is a fact that those with a vested interest in the continuing rivalry between east and west will find direly significant.

In 1115 Prince David, heir to the Scottish throne, founded the See of Glasgow. His tutor, John Achaius, the new bishop, obviously felt the old wood and wattle church of Saint Mungo did not sit well with his dignity, and in 1124 he began a building of wood and stone. It was destroyed by fire in 1192, but was restored by the great Bishop Joceline and re-opened in 1197.

Perhaps because we were exposed to *The Pickwick Papers* at an early age we are naturally sceptical of stones bearing inscriptions. The stone in a wall in the Cathedral grounds is no exception. At first we wondered if the coat of arms might be that of the archbishop at the time, but this theory ran slap into the fact that for twenty-three years from 1638 there were none. Further research unearthed that in May 1657 Glasgow took possession 'of an ingyne for casting water on land that is on fyre' and from then boasted its own fire engine. A matter for civic pride, no doubt, but hardly to this extent. At this point we gave up and withdrew to a bench in Glasgow Green.

Here we could look over at the Doulton Fountain (left), a born-again relic of Victorian arrogance. Originally part of the International Exhibition of 1888 in Kelvingrove Park, it shows Queen Victoria surmounting the various and varied people of empire, and was described with typical Victorian modesty as 'the most astonishing piece of earthenware ever made'. It was shifted to Glasgow Green in 1890, and the following year a bolt of lightning struck it and totally destroyed the queen. When the city fathers proposed replacing her with an urn, Mr Doulton, outraged by this creeping republicanism, replaced the statue at his own expense.

That observant gentleman, Francois, duc de la Rochefoucauld, seems to have ended up like all observant gentlemen, with a somewhat sour view of the human race. Funereal pomp, he considered, has more to do with the vanity of the living than with honouring the dead. This brings him in line with current thought, which considers the Victorians were cannibalistic in the meal they made of mortality, and may be what pigeons try to convey via any statue of any once-celebrated nonentity. And even a fall of snow can add its own disrespectful comment. Instead of turning the funereal pomp in the above corner of the Glasgow Necropolis into a winter wonderland, it transforms a dark angel into a Glasgow coalman brooding on the iniquity of having to tote a bag of nutty slack up four flights of stairs.

John K. McDowall in *The People's History of Glasgow,* which was published in 1899, claimed that Glasgow had about one hundred cranes in the harbour 'with lifts varying from 35 cwts to 130 tons'. In 1899, this was obviously something to crow about, but nowadays it is just another sad statistic, and the cranes have declined with the river. One Sunday morning, we were staring out of a window in the house we then lived in, which had a splendid view of the river, when there came a loud bang, and a crane began slowly to collapse, sinking to the ground like some great wounded mechanical animal. Three cranes went down that morning, and the fact that it was a Sunday made this crane cull seem something sacriligious.

The Clyde made Glasgow and Glasgow made the Clyde, as the old saying has it. Now Glasgow is remaking the Clyde, and the three cranes we mentioned were victims of this process. As was the Queen's Dock, which was filled in with rubble from the demolished St Enoch's Hotel. This made us feel rather uneasy, like watching compulsory cannibalism. The seagulls are apparently unperturbed by the whole business, but it is later than they think. Where the Queen's Dock used to be, helicopters are already landing.

The social scientists call it 'defensive space'. We are not quite sure what it is exactly, and have no intention of finding out since next week those same social scientists will have come up with something else. But as far as we can make out, it is one of those phenomena that can only be explained negatively. This technique, you will recall, was pioneered by Saint Thomas Aquinas, who defined evil as the absence of good, which anyone could have told him and which does not take us much farther.

Anyway, the passengers on the *Waverley* are huddled together because they have too much space, and too much space is hostile because it makes you feel small. And you know what happens to small things, don't you? Sea serpents eat them, that's what.

The people standing at the bus stop in Bath Street seem to have varying ideas about how much space is defensive. The three women at the head of the queue seem to have it made and to be quite happy about their space allocation. The man in the middle seems unhappy, but to judge by his attitude would be unhappy anyway about anything. The man on his left is worried because his space is being encroached on by the young lady with the bright red hold-all. The man and woman at the end of the line are apparently comfortable and have plenty of room, which is maybe what 'defensive space' means. The man at the extreme left is in the wrong queue.

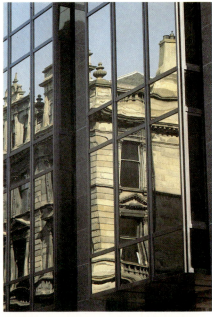

History is sometimes curiously blind, or perhaps just plain capricious in its selection of those to be remembered. In a city described as possessing the most underrated Victorian architecture in Europe, the two most familiar architectural names as far as the layman is concerned are Charles Rennie Mackintosh and Alexander 'Greek' Thomson, both of whom would appear to be architectural mavericks. Yet the mainstream practitioners are worthy of note, and even the most conventional of these is capable of a flash of genius, poetry, daftness, call it what you will. William Leiper, a quiet, shy man, has his monument on Glasgow Green (opposite, below right) in the shape of an outburst of Paduan Gothic, a copy of the Doge's Palace in Venice, once a carpet factory now a small business centre. Gomme and Walker, in *The Architecture of Glasgow,* call it a 'weird *tour de force*', yet under snow and humanized by the two figures in the foreground, it evokes a scene from *Doctor Zhivago.* Not surprising perhaps when one recalls that the Kremlin was built to the design of Italian architects.

Charles Wilson was a prolific practitioner and a designer of spacious, opulent houses for spacious, opulent people, as in Kirklee Terrace (left). He, too, was a quiet, shy man. Perhaps that explains the Italian influence on him and Leiper, or was it a necessary condition of tender?

Another forgotten Glasgow architect was James Salmon Junior, who designed the building at 142 St Vincent Street (top left), which is known to Glaswegians as The Hatrack and which in its solution to the problem of minimal space recalls Amsterdam. It is buttressed now by an insurance company's building, which provides a looking glass for its neighbours (top right). Salmon was known by his fellow professionals as the Wee Troot, which suggests that architects have a sense of humour, but not much.

We've forgotten who that poet was who sighed 'O for a little tobacconist's shop!' but we have always found his choice of shop significant. Not for him a butcher's, a baker's, or a candlestick-maker's. He is quite specific about the kind of shop he wants. And we feel instinctively that he was right. There has always been a rapport between literature and tobacco. It was originally introduced into Britain by a man who was a better writer than he was an explorer, and long after Raleigh had been executed, the weed that he brought back from the New World made Glasgow rich and some of its population insufferable.

Perhaps some of the assumption of the Tobacco Lords that they were not as other people has rubbed off on tobacconists' shops. The overweening arrogance of the men who trod the Plainstanes has been transmuted into a genteel superiority, and the ladies behind the counters know that Sir James Barrie was on their side and that the colourful figure with his straw hat, blue jacket with brass buttons, yellow trousers and scarlet cummerbund is quite harmless, being on leave from a Currier and Ives print.

Glasgow's patron saint is Saint Mungo, alias Kentigern, whose father was a prince of Strathclyde and whose mother was the daughter of a Saxon king with the vaguely republican name — for a monarch — of Loth. Mungo probably founded the church in Glasgow and probably did a lot of other things, but facts about him are few. Legends, however, can be as revealing. One in particular, concerning the tale of an erring wife and how Mungo miraculously saved her reputation with the aid of a fish, indicates a degree of tolerance unusual in a Scottish churchman.

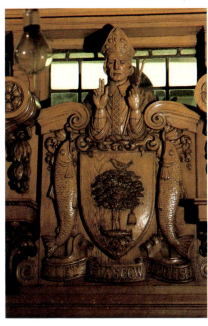

Perhaps it is a mistake to lump all the Tobacco Lords together and to dismiss them offhand as a gang of plutocrats and philistines. That many of them deserved both these epithets cannot be gainsaid, but there are always exceptions to prove any rule. In Scotland, men of family seem to have had no snobbish inhibitions about trade as an unworthy occupation for gentlemen. One authority says this of them: '. . . existing contacts within the community and a measure of wealth were normally vital if the aspirant was to achieve the desired goal of partnership status. Thus, newcomers tended to come from the "middling" ranks of Lowland Scottish society. While none were scions of the aristocracy, only a mere handful were the sons of skilled craftsmen. Most were the offspring of merchants, lairds, and professional families.'

Walter Stirling, who left a thousand pounds and a collection of 804 books to found the first public library in Glasgow, was the son of a surgeon, and his munificence finally found a permanent home in the Royal Exchange Building which incorporates part of the former town house of another Tobacco Lord, William Cunninghame, who had forked out ten thousand pounds for it. The incorporation was carried out by David Hamilton, whose definition of incorporation would have met with the approval of a boa constrictor since it appears to have swallowed up the Cunninghame mansion entirely.

David Hamilton has another, if rather peripheral, claim to fame. At one time he was the partner — briefly — of James Smith, whose daughter Madeleine had the leading role in one of the most celebrated murder trials of Victorian times.

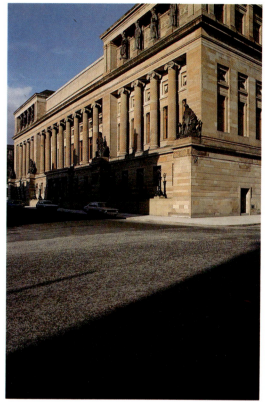

All over Glasgow are buildings which bear witness to an earlier age's almost touching faith in the magical properties of education, or at least in the printed word, which may be a different thing. In these days of Munn and Dunning, when a whole new concept of education is being hotly debated, the old certainties no longer seem so authoritative, or so monolithic. Yet it is surprising how durable they proved to be and how many people are prepared to defend them even now. The lad o' pairts is a cherished figure in Scottish educational mythology, the poverty-stricken youth walking immense distances to university, carrying a bag of oatmeal to ward off starvation successfully, if monotonously, for a whole session. The way things are going nowadays, the modern lad o' pairts will have to replace the traditional oatmeal with gold dust, now that the grant system is under attack.

All this, of course, lay hidden in the future when Stephen Mitchell, a tobacco baron of the nineteenth century, left the money for a large public library. The Mitchell Library has become a repository of Old Glasgow while managing to accommodate the new. It is enshrined in the memories of thousands of ex-students, now middle-aged and as mature as they will ever be. The back of the building houses a beautiful little theatre where you can see amateur performances of *South Pacific* or earnest productions by the kind of companies which have been aptly described by someone or other as 'left-wing hitch-hikers'.

We asked our old friend Simon Ersatz, the celebrated art critic of the *Sunday Waffle,* to comment on the pictures to the left. Here is what he wrote:

'Emerson did not take his degree at Harvard because, as he said, he did not think it was worth five dollars. He never gave any reasons for this assessment, and perhaps, in this instance, reasons are irrelevant, the real importance being the gesture itself and the exciting precedent it sets for those of us who have the country's aesthetic reputation in our keeping.

'It has long been an open secret that, once they are outside the safety of the groves of Academe, academics tend to lose even the most minimal aesthetic judgement. Perhaps the assumption that they have any is unwarranted. If they had, they would probably not be academics. But I am in danger of mounting a hobby horse . . .

'I understand that the top picture shows the University of Strathclyde flanked by the sculptures that await my comments. As you know, sculpture has NEVER been my favourite medium, and I confess that these particular examples leave me strangely unmoved. I keep seeing them as badly moored gondolas, which is a TERRIBLY literary reaction. My friend Torquil says they evoke for him two Easter Island statues chatting up two other Easter Island statues. The bottom picture shows the new library at the University of Glasgow and demonstrates what happens when architects flirt with rough trade and clients allow them that privilege because they don't know any better.

'In conclusion, may I say that my own alma mater never made the kind of mistakes illustrated. Torquil says the reason for that is that the Fine Arts department was kept too busy recruiting for the KGB.'

Glasgow is filled with strange little details, some ensconced in museums, others taking their chances in the open air. Bishop Blackadder's chair in the Hunterian Museum, once used to time the discourses of unhappy students, has no doubt been superseded by a chair with a built-in digital watch.

The staircase in the University of Glasgow's Bute Hall still retains a fine phoney medievalness that is oddly cinematic. The lion and the

unicorn appear to be worried because that well-known Transylvanian aristocrat has not come home yet, and here it is daylight. Perhaps he could do with a digital watch too.

The Mackintosh detail on the Glasgow School of Art is less exotic. Unlike Count Dracula, the railings take advantage of the daylight, turning a shaft of sunlight into an almost audible harp *glissando*.

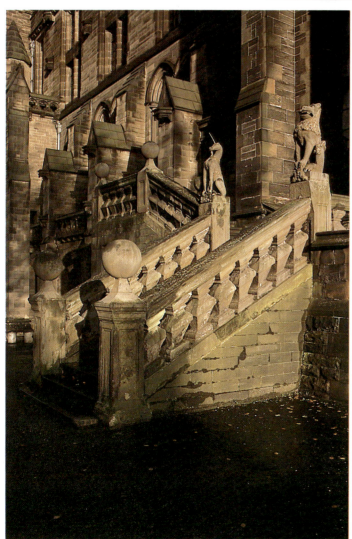

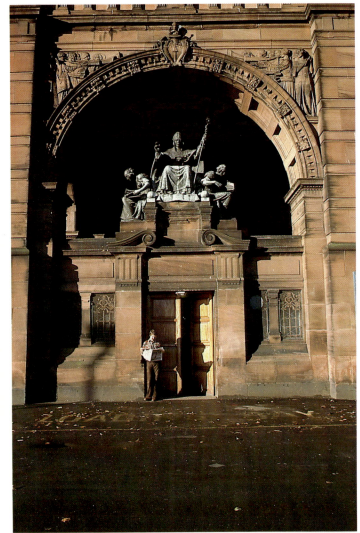

In Paris, the Opéra had its
phantom, so let us not grudge
Glasgow's main museum its legend.
This has it that Kelvingrove Art
Gallery and Museum was built the
wrong way round. When this fact
was pointed out to the architect, he
did the only thing an honourable
ARIBA could do. He climbed to the
highest point of the misplaced
museum, and with a wild cry
hurled himself into outer space.
The stone gentleman in the
foreground believes the story
implicitly. He himself was blown
into the River Kelvin in 1941 and
lay there for nine years before being
rescued and restored.

   The man in the picture on his
right is reading his newspaper at
the back of the building, or perhaps
at the front if you believe the
legend. Meanwhile, inside the
Gallery an anxious dominie checks
up and discovers that three of his
party have gone adrift. They are
downstairs in the gun room,
plotting a bank robbery ten years
from now. They will carry it out
disguised as highwaymen and have
just discovered where to get the
necessary pistols. Back upstairs, the
Scottish Colourists come under
expert and detailed scrutiny, while,
right across the city, at the Burrell
Collection gallery, patrons of the
restaurant are reminded that a good
lunch can be a work of art.

A busman's holiday at the Glasgow Transport Museum. A railwayman is properly reverential — or is perhaps simply bowed down — beneath the weight of regal railway relics. It is just possible, of course, that he is a latterday Jacobite, wondering where the railway engine was when Bonnie Prince Charlie really needed it.

In the Thirties, everything the Hollywood Dream Factory produced was avidly consumed by Glaswegians, who, at that time, had something like 130 cinemas. The halcyon days of Hollywood may be over, but the great days of Glasgow as a cinema city, in an active way, may only be beginning. Already, foreign directors have recognized the photogenic qualities of the city, and with the emergence of an increasingly successful native industry, Kelvin Drive leading to Botanic Crescent might one day be as well known as Sunset and Vine.

People who live in glass houses are traditionally warned against throwing stones. Turning into stone, however, is a different matter, and if your taste runs to see-through domiciles, all you have to do is get petrified and the city fathers will rush to see that you are suitably housed. This particular glass house is in Victoria Park and contains the famous Fossil Grove. One small boy who obviously did not believe in fossils insisted that he intended to wait until the elephants came back to collect their feet.

There has always been an element of fantasy in the term 'winter garden', especially in a country where winter means a halt to work in the garden. It may have been, therefore, a kind of pragmatism that led to the neglect by the city fathers of the Winter Gardens at the People's Palace. Perhaps they associated winter gardens with places like Bournemouth, seaside and seasonal, while here they were trying to drag into the twentieth century a city still in shock from the Industrial Revolution. And the people who might have provided a corrective to this attitude were trapped in their own snobberies which boiled down to a certain kind of light music, tinkling tea cups, and boring conversations about the old days in some hill station or other in India.

To record that all is now well would be premature. The local government's attitude may be more enlightened, but the Winter Gardens — perhaps winter gardens everywhere — are still an endangered species. The new threat is from central government, whose financially stringent policies put all such places at risk. It would be the height of irony if they were bundled into limbo by a government which most people associate with a certain kind of light music, tinkling tea cups, and boring conversations about the old days in some hill station or other in India.

Among our papers, which we are hoarding for posterity, there is a sheet bearing the following lines in our own illegible handwriting:

In W2 did Wee McCann
A stately pleasure dome decree
Where Kelvin, sacred river, ran
Through caverns measureless
   to man,
Down to the BBC.

We should like to make it clear (in case we are unlucky in our biographer) that these lines represent a donnish joke. Wee McCann is a figment of our imagination, and although the Kelvin does actualy run down to the BBC, just the width of a road from where the picture was taken, the poem is actually a parody of 'Kubla Khan', a very much anthologized work by Samuel Taylor Coleridge (not to be confused with Samuel Coleridge Taylor, who wrote music).

The truth of the matter is that the stately pleasure dome on the left is the Kibble Palace in the Botanic Gardens. Originally part of Mr John Kibble's estate at Coulport on Loch Long, it is actually younger, in a Glasgow context, than Coleridge's famous poem. Mr Kibble's palace arrived at Kelvinside in 1871, by which time Coleridge had been dead for almost forty years.

Some authorities are categorical about it. Pollok House, they say, is an Adam building. An official leaflet, published by Glasgow Museums, seems to hedge its bets by saying that the central block was 'once thought to be the work of the architects William and John Adam'. Agreement appears to be general that the central block dates back to about 1750. This gives it a claim to charm and elegance, since for the eighteenth century these are the automatic nouns. Our own view is that the eighteenth century has had a ridiculously good press. Academics as well as writers of the Jeffrey Farnol/Georgette Heyer school have surrounded it with a halo of romance that plays down such unpleasant realities as public executions, brutal bare-knuckle prize fights, and bear baiting. When Pollok House was built — whoever built it — Glasgow was a city of small shopkeepers, who, compared say with Londoners, lived in a state of primeval innocence. Or if you prefer it in Marxist terms, Glasgow was at the stage of primitive accumulation, which is another way of saying that the small shopkeepers were stashing the loot away so that in due course they could become big Tobacco Lords.

In 1892, long after the Tobacco Lords had gone to join those other casualties of over-specialization, the dinosaurs, Sir John Stirling Maxwell, the tenth baronet, decided to make his contribution to Pollok. To assist him, he enlisted Robert Rowand Anderson, who designed the additional wings, the entrance hall, and service area, with a respect for the original that bordered on a subjugation of his own artistic personality. Never one to do things by halves, Sir John moved in paintings from his father's collection. This is especially strong in Spanish paintings, whose merits were recognized by Sir John's father at a time when they were generally undervalued and, therefore, presumably, underpriced.

Having sorted out the inside of the house to his satisfaction, Sir John moved out into the open air. Sir John it was who landscaped the gardens, and we like to think it was he who planted the Virginia creeper that covers the wall of the little garden pavilion and makes a satirical comment on the men who walked the Plainstanes, their arrogance ablaze in scarlet cloaks.

Pollok House was gifted to Glasgow by Mrs Anne Maxwell Macdonald and her family in 1966.

Once the image was wet afternoons and surly attendants, bored children and even more bored teachers. Two depressing climates, one physical, the other mental. It is ludicrous to suggest that the physical climate has changed, despite grandma's conviction that it's all down to them atom bomb tests. The mental climate, however, has. Museums seem brighter now and more organized, less like a hyperactive jackdaw's nest; and whatever your interest is there's a museum to cater for it, even if it's a cotoneaster at Pollok House or a Glasgow Style rose everywhere you look. We ourself were thrilled to find in the Transport Museum a model of the ship in which our parent spent many years sailing between Ardrossan and Belfast. We half expected to find him still in it, suitably reduced to scale.

This made us wonder about the men in charge of the boating ponds in Strathclyde's parks. Is this one, at Rouken Glen, fully qualified and holding a master's ticket? Does he know the difference between fore, main, and mizzen? Could he wear a ship on a lee shore? Or was he simply chosen because he can be heard above a force 8 gale: 'Come in, Number Six. Your time is UP!'

We have always thought of Glasgow as a museum-loving city, ever since, shortly after we settled in the city, we saw an incredible sight. It was 1946. There were crowds queuing to get into the Art Gallery, and when we say crowds we mean the kind of numbers that would gladden the heart of a provincial football club's treasurer, or at least his bank manager. Day after day these queues stretched from the entrance on to Sauchiehall Street and continued for more than a hundred yards down that famous thoroughfare. It was the size of crowd that now might assemble to glimpse an over-publicized pop star, and even then might have gathered to see a siren of the silver screen. Yet what had brought these crowds to wait patiently in the spring sunshine was an exhibition by two artists, Matisse and Picasso. The star was Picasso's celebrated *Guernica,* which probably had an extra impact on people whose first-hand experience of the Luftwaffe was still fresh and vivid. We have always remembered those queues, sometimes with a faint disbelief. They had an innocence we shall probably never see again, and the uneasy thought at times surfaces that the innocence was in ourself.

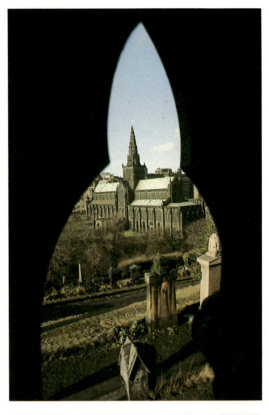

'The quickest way to establish and build up an inferiority complex is to be continually faced by excellence.'

'But doesn't continual excellence run the danger of becoming boring?'

'Not to an inferiority complex.'

'This debate is degenerating into a circular argument.'

'Strange things an inferiority complex can get up to. Coping with excellence, I mean.'

'I have the kind of mind that needs concrete examples.'

'Right. Take the pictures on this page.'

'Douglas Corrance has already taken them.'

'All right, clever Dick. Which one is odd one out?'

'This is you coping with excellence?'

'Exactly. But you haven't answered the question.'

'Let me see now. I quite like that shot of the Cathedral as the Hunchback of Notre Dame might have seen it.'

'Go on.'

'Or that infantryman's view of Queen Victoria in George Square.'

'You're not even getting warm.'

'Is that Saint George's Tron Church reflected in that glass?'

'It is indeed.'

'And surely that must be Queen's Cross Church, the only church that Mackintosh designed.'

'Right again. But you're obviously not going to come up with the answer, so you might as well give up. The odd one out is Queen Victoria. All the others show churches. The statue spoils the sequence.'

'And you call that coping with excellence?'

'Yes. How else would you describe it?'

'How about nit-picking?'

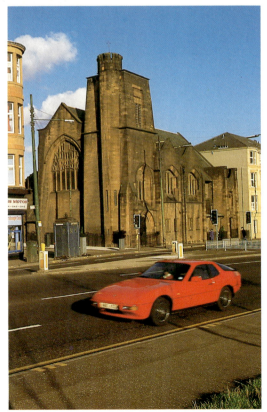

This house is somewhere in Garnethill. All you have to do is search around until you find a place that is frozen in time. Do you remember copper coal scuttles? Fairings that stood proudly on the mantelpiece? Patterned wallpaper? Lace curtains that were probably woven in Darvel, Ayrshire? Clothes with hundreds of minute buttons waiting to be sent into oblivion by the zip fastener? The sound of the clock chiming every fifteen minutes? The long bolster on the brass bed?

The rooms have the strangeness of the *Marie Celeste*. Someone has just stepped out for a minute, will be back soon. There's time to poke around in their life, time to wonder about its familiarity and its utter strangeness. How did people live in those days? What were their thoughts, their hopes, their fears? You hear the clock ticking, then the realization dawns, an intimation of mortality, that no one will ever be coming back again to hear its familiar chime.

Symbols are tricky things to handle. And if it is true, as Karl Jaspers says it is, that anything can become a symbol at any moment, then the need for caution is as obvious as it is difficult. The cardinal principle would appear to be that oil and water do not mix.

The burglar alarm, symbol *par excellence* of materialism, when placed beside a pious sentiment becomes something entirely new, a cynical comment on both materialism and a certain kind of piety.

Originally, one could argue, there were no doors since people who lived in caves apparently felt no need of them. Who thought of the first door is not recorded, and its significance is still a matter for discussion. Did the first door mark a new awareness of self, or was it simply a shield against prowling sabre-toothed tigers? Whatever it was, doors were soon here to stay, while sabre-toothed tigers proved redundant, evolution-wise.

Our own interest in doors can be traced back to a favourite uncle, who was an Edgar Wallace buff and who, as far as we remember, never read a book that was written by anyone else. The books were passed on to us, and by the age of ten we had read the whole Edgar Wallace *oeuvre*. Wallace, too, had a thing about doors, especially doors like the green one with the patchwork notices of small tailors and those in the garment trade generally. Wallace stories are filled with doors like that, which, sooner or later, the hero opens to reveal exquisite rooms that cost a king's ransom to furnish. This usually happens in the penultimate chapter.

The white door with the vaguely eastern flavour is definitely more upmarket. The plant in the foreground is waiting for a reply from the Ansaphone, and when it comes the plant will reply, 'Mr Macbeth. This is Birnam Wood from Dunsinane.'

The remaining door is a Mackintosh door from the Willow Tearoom, now lovingly restored in Sauchiehall Street.

All over the city we come across
unexpected little flashes of colour
making their mildly defiant
statements or modestly underlining
a statement by someone else.
Through the severe verticals of the
Willow Tearoom we seem to catch a
rainbow standing to attention.
Lenten lilies wave a regal and
seasonal greeting to George Square
from the City Chambers. And in
Garnethill, the coloured horizontals
interpose themselves to try and
soften the severity of the roadway.
And fail.

Yesterday is in today's window. Come in and browse around. We sell
yesterday, but don't let that give you ideas. There are bits of yesterday that
are not for sale.

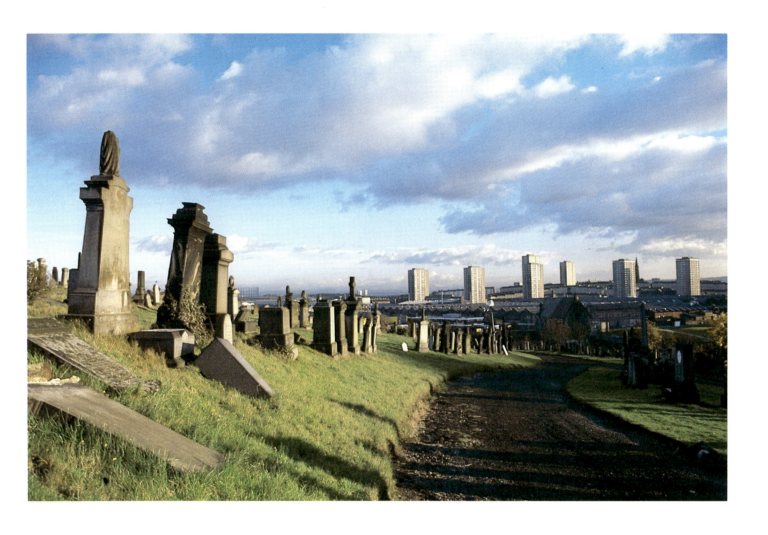

What manner of men they were
Who shall be declaring?
The ancient, crumbled stone
Stares across at the raw northern newness,
But the message is silent.

Our day is gone,
As one day so will yours.
It is happening now,
As we stare at each other
Beneath the house of the lark.

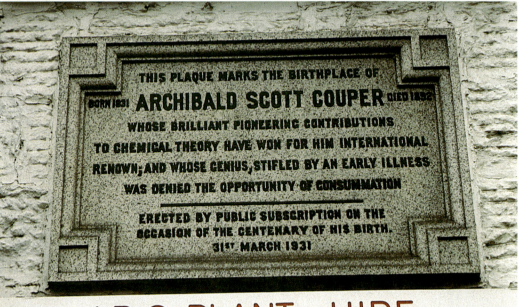

J.B.S. PLANT HIRE   776.0455

For all Kirkintilloch's right to fame as a Roman fort on the Antonine Wall, with an ancient name derived from two forms of Celtic — *Caer-penn-taloch,* 'the stronghold on the end of the ridge' — Kirkie is too often better known for its forty-eight dry years, when it had no public houses.

Prohibition came to Scotland in piecemeal fashion in 1913, when the Temperance (Scotland) Act allowed local communities to veto the issuing of licences for the sale of alcohol. The supporters of the Temperance Society and the Band of Hope made their veto effective in 1920, and the last call for last orders was in 1921. Large majorities at later polls gave no indication of the surprising reverse there would be in 1968, when the majority voted for repeal, and Kirkintilloch rejoined the wets.

Archibald Scott Couper's right to fame had been completely forgotten until a German scientist, intrigued by the sudden disappearance of this genius, researched the details of his sad life. Because, in 1858, the French Academy deliberately delayed Couper's presentation of his theory on molecular structure by three months, his career as a chemist declined into obscurity and insanity, while the other runner in the race, Kekulé von Stradonitz, moved on to academic honour and success.

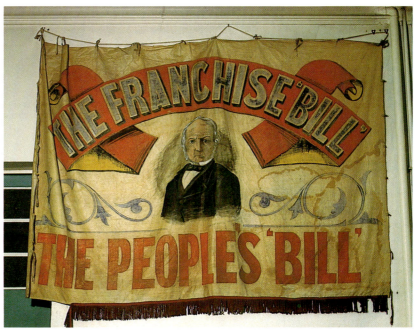

Agitation for reform has a long tradition in Kilsyth. These banners are in the chapel of Colzium House on the outskirts of Kilsyth and now a community centre. The 'four pounders' which threatened the House of Lords were householders whose rates were four pounds in 1810. Mr Gladstone's Electoral Reform Bill won Kilsyth's support in 1884. The Brotherhood was devoted to Pleasant Sunday Afternoons, for men only, and they met for moral and spiritual reform in the early 1900s.

Art nouveau came to Kilsyth as a quiet place for people to meet and talk, take tea and coffee, cakes and biscuits, and measure out life with sugar tongs. Today, in Dawson's Bakery, the same art nouveau decor screens the queue for cakes and biscuits. The talk is just as crisp and tart, sometimes sugary, even spicy, but if they want tea or coffee with their pineapple tarts they must wait until they go home.

In Cumbernauld, not so much a cottage, more a Cottage Theatre and an active and enterprising one at that. Where workers once lived, players now play to create illusion; where workers now live, in factory-built houses, factory-built panels of pine and panelled doors create their own illusion of difference.

We must admit that our reflections on the fairly young town of Cumbernauld are based on experiences when it was still a fairly new town. One of the guiding principles of the planners (if planners can be said to be guided) was that the new residents of Cumbernauld should be safe from traffic accidents. There is no way to stop some drivers bumping their cars into things, but if pedestrians never cross roads and cars never cross the paths of pedestrians, they are unlikely to bump into each other. However, at the times when a driver would like to bump into a pedestrian, in a manner of speaking, pedestrians are never to be found. Cumbernauld certainly does not have as many roundabouts or empty anonymous roads as Milton Keynes, but b.m.k. (before Milton Keynes) Cumbernauld was the place for roundabouts and empty roads; no people, just roundabouts and roads. No one for the disorientated driver to ask, 'Can you tell me where . . .?'

This is certainly not the question the woman is asking the child.

Parents, if parent she be, are more direct. 'Where have you been — without your clothes on?' This mother seems permanently surprised to see this child: universal mother, universal child. 'Am I yours? Are you mine?' There is a tension, if not a question, between these two figures.

The good people of Cumbernauld politely ignore this eternal domestic dispute. They get on with carrying home the bacon, paying the rent on the video, discussing the football last week, this week, forever. All this social to and fro takes place in streets, or walks, safe from cars and lorries, buses and taxis, wind and rain, and sunshine. There is some sunlight but no sunshine. Perhaps that is the child's answer to the mother's question. The child has been sunbathing in the car park. But not on the day when the two old friends met there. That day had typical Strathclyde weather — mild, dull, and a hint of rain. Just the weather to encourage a few ghostly cars to materialize among the real things.

The splendid imperial eagle in Airdrie's coat of arms, symbol of the authority of the Roman emperors and of all emperors since, is drawn from a branch of the local landowning family, the Aitchisons (or Achesons, as they once were). One of their number, trailing his coat, was known, in Armagh, as Monteagle of Monteagle.

If you are happy at your work, the world is a better place. If your work makes the world a better place, you have achieved much. Many would argue that we should alter our attitudes to work since many of us now have none. A careful look at our happy band in Airdrie will show that the man in overalls is the worker — he has a real job. He had it last week, last month, last year. He has always had a job. Next week and next year are a different matter. The likely lads are trainees, although whether they are training to do jobs or to do without jobs is something they do not seem inclined to contemplate.

Tom Ellis has transformed his own and his neighbour's council-house gardens in Airdrie into such a splendid blaze of colour that people now beat a path to his door.

Airdrie's splendid coat of arms, with the Aitchison cock on top, has here become the war mask of some fierce king supported by two medieval knights. All three warriors are reminiscent of the Teutonic knights created by Sergei Eisenstein in his film *Alexander Nevski*. Their watchfulness echoes the town motto — *Vigilantibus*, 'while they watch'.

Among all this tartan splendour in Airdrie market, it is interesting that the real clothes on the real people have drawn on influences much farther afield than Sir Walter Scott's kailyard.

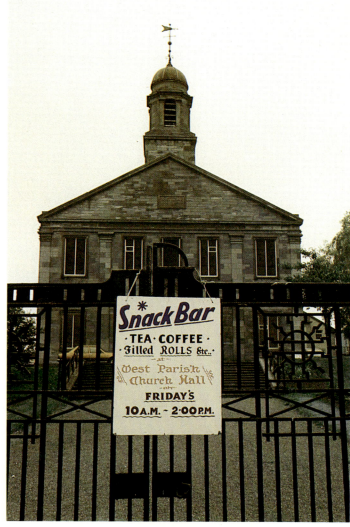

There is just a hint of doubt about this use of Airdrie's West Parish Church Hall. Compare the lettering in its notice with the cheery, simple confidence of CHICKEN PUDDING TEA.

Coatbridge has given its wide main street to the pedestrians among its population. The modern development has its echo in the simple lines on the left and in the lamp standards. The terrace on the right with its clock has an echo of cartwheels on cobbles. The gaudy fascias of the ground-floor shops echo the brash Sixties, when petrol, credit, and cars were cheap.

Bothwell has a much more respectable nature than you would expect from its fiery history. The once-splendid castle was the home of the tempestuous Earl of Bothwell, third husband of Mary, Queen of Scots. A bridge still crosses the Clyde where the Covenanters fought and died in defence of their view of religious liberty, but its significance is now lost in a swirl of roundabouts leading to and from the M74 motorway.

The key to the future of the folk of Wishaw, among other places, lies in that skyline. Should Ravenscraig steelworks ever suffer the fate of Bothwell Castle. . . .

At Hamilton
lie the heads of
JOHN PARKER, GAVIN HAMILTON,
JAMES HAMILTON,
and
CHRISTOPHER STRANG,
who suffered at
EDINBURGH
Decr 7th 1666.

Stay, passenger take notice
what thou reads!
At Edinburgh lie our bodies,
here our heads;
Our right hands stood at Lanark
these we want,
Because with them we sware
the Covenant.

The Old Parish Church of Hamilton is shaped like a Celtic cross, with four identical entrances linked to a circular centre. The clock tower, reminiscent of many in central London, is above an Italianate portico. This is the second parish church of Hamilton. In 1734, the then Duke of Hamilton wanted sole use of the medieval church as a family vault. William Adam, who had just designed a little place in France for the Duke, who is also Duc de Chatelherault, designed this church to replace the original, which has been deliberately knocked about a bit to make it look more romantic.

The flat memorial stones protected the dead from those who

THE BATTLE OF THE HIETON

WAS FOUGHT ON THE BANKS OF THIS STREAM
BETWEEN
THE COVENANTERS UNDER COLONEL KER
AND
THE ENGLISH UNDER GENERAL LAMBERT
IN 1650

ERECTED BY
THE HAMILTON AND DISTRICT CIVIC SOCIETY

would have robbed them. One memorial stone in the churchyard predates the church itself. The memorial to the four Covenanters was probably raised after 1690 and moved to the wall of the new churchyard. Comparison of the dates of the Battle of Hieton — a burn which flows through Hamilton to the Clyde — the execution of the four men, and the Battle of Bothwell Brig gives some idea of the extent of the civil war in the southwest of Scotland between the signing of the Covenant in 1634 and 1690. The savage death of these four Covenanters was a fate such zealots inflicted on their own victims during these bitter, religious times.

The twentieth century was only a few weeks from its bloody birth with the First World War when, on 9 July 1914, King George V formally opened what is now the Hamilton District Council Central Offices. Town council architecture had not then thrown off the influence of its Victorian heyday, and this building is none the worse for that.

The Hamilton family seems to have had a preoccupation with resting places for the deceased, or perhaps many deceased to cater for. The lions which guard the Mausoleum have something in common with the miners who used the safety lamps now in Hamilton District Museum. While this lion sleeps, the other is wide awake.

The Mausoleum is all that remains of Hamilton Palace, the seat of the family. Built in the 1820s, it had to be demolished in 1927 after mine workings — the source of the Hamilton money — made the building unsafe.

One of the most successful creations of local government planners in the 1970s was Strathclyde Country Park. Lying alongside the Clyde between Hamilton and Motherwell, it is a splendid place to sit, walk, sail, run, play games, or just soak up the sun and the elixir of youth.

If our three men in a boat knew the secret of the Hamilton Mausoleum, also in Strathclyde Park, in the policies below the Race Course, they could make a grand noise. Built by the tenth Duke of Hamilton in 1840, it has an echo, echo, echo, echo . . .

This nineteenth-century Scottish living room is in the eighteenth-century mill tenement in Blantyre where the Victorian hero, David Livingstone, was born, lived, and studied medicine. We were told, especially when we complained about going to school, that he walked to and from Glasgow University every day, a distance of twelve miles. This was good preparation for walking halfway across Africa — several times. When he came upon the Cloud that Thunders on the Zambezi River, he renamed it Victoria Falls. Patriotism he had, imagination he lacked.

In 1769, the tenth Earl of Eglinton and Winton, Alexander Montgomerie, decided to rebuild the village of Eaglesham. These neat two-storey houses have changed little since then. A few new houses were added after the train and bus brought Eaglesham within easy reach of Glasgow, but further development has been strictly controlled.

The skyline beyond Eaglesham shows another new development, East Kilbride New Town. Based on the village of East Kilbride, which had the first Scottish cotton mill in 1783, the new town was started in 1948. The sculpted musician behind the sculpted hairstyle should ideally have an electric guitar. The future of East Kilbride — at one end of Silicon Glen — lies in electronics.

High up in the Lanarkshire hills winter comes early to Strathaven (pronounced Str'aven) and stays late. It is perhaps for this reason that, having been cut off by the elements, it cut itself off from its neighbours. In the *Third Statistical Account of Scotland,* published in 1952, the local minister records the insularity of his parishioners with patience and sympathy. Even that recently it was still possible to be considered an incomer, however many years had been spent in the village, if you had not actually been born there. Yet, by the 1950s, Strathaven had been within easy access of Glasgow and Hamilton for some time. Buses took an hour to come from Glasgow and only half an hour from Hamilton. Incomers had seen and admired Strathaven. Some had been determined enough to stay. Others came back each summer.

Due to this combination of fierce pride in what they had and the enthusiasm of the incomers for their new home, Strathaven has undergone a recent revival, and its town mill is now a new arts centre where 'for quality better canna be'.

It does not matter how many caber lengths it is from the Highland Line of old to Carmunnock. If a Lowland village has a claim to hold its own Highland Games, then Carmunnock's claim is as good as any. Perched on the side of Cathkin Braes, Carmunnock has a clear view across Glasgow to the Campsie Fells and beyond Dumgoyne to the peaks of Ben Arthur, Ben Vorlich, Ben Venue, Ben Lomond, and Ben More.

There was a time when village life in Carmunnock was declining under pressure from the attractions offered by Glasgow. If community spirits can be raised by the organization of the Highland Games, then more power to their elbows, wrists, shoulders, backs, or knees, or whatever else is needed to make a telegraph pole tum'le its wilkies, or a village community revive interest in itself.

It may just be fun and games to some folk, but it takes a great deal of concentration to remember all the steps of the Highland Fling. You have to close your eyes and bite your lip, make sure your fingers are in the right position, and then you can imagine all the different steps, and when the music starts it's as simple as a log falling over.

When there is all the fun of the fair to be enjoyed, who cares whether it originated with the celebration of the summer solstice or Corpus Christi processions. Time is just a Big Wheel which has been turning for Lanark since it was a Roman camp, hence the ever-watchful eagle on the town crest.

The bell in the claw of the eagle of Lanark may represent the silver bell given to the town by William the Lyon as a prize for a horse race, the oldest such trophy in the world and competed for at Lanark every autumn until 1976. The silver bell, now in Clydesdale District's safekeeping, so to speak, is a seventeenth-century replica, but the Lanimer, or land-marking procession, is much older. The original idea was to ride round the marches, or marks, of the town so that everyone would know what was inside, and outside. All this is no longer necessary, but every town should have a reason for an annual celebration, and the older the reason the better. In Lanark, the Cornet (he is the one with the flag) has been leading the local riders out of the town and around the marks at the beginning of June for over one hundred years. Looks well for his age. . . .

New Lanark, on the banks of the Clyde, was founded in 1786 by David Dale and Richard Arkwright as a cotton-milling village. Surprisingly perhaps, many of the original work force were Highlanders, their graves now among the trees on the left. Dale could not persuade the local farm labourers to come to work in his new-fangled factory, so when he heard of a destitute party of Highlanders stranded at Greenock after the ship taking them to a new life in North America was wrecked, he offered them work, shelter, and a future. The turret-shaped building was the general office from which Robert Owen, Dale's son-in-law and an active reformer, organized the village and mill.

One river is much like any other,
Only water pushing water
Ever onwards, endless.
Each river has its lands,
Its history, its people and its moods.
Something there is in me loves
This river. It rattles rapidly across the rocks

Between tall walls of green,
Forces foaming past the stoney banks
And leaves behind a quiet roar
On warm drowsy summer days as
Swaying wasps whisper and seduce and
Large black still pools reflect
Little white ducks.

The name Biggar could mean 'the bend in the Clyde' (*big* or *bege*), or 'the bog land' (*big thir*). Both watery features identify the village. Its agricultural heyday is well reflected in the Gladstone Court Street Museum where the grocer's shop still waits for your valued custom. Its history is displayed in the seventeenth-century Greenhill Covenanter's House, formerly a ruined farmhouse which was moved stone by stone ten miles from its original site. The horse made it under his own power.

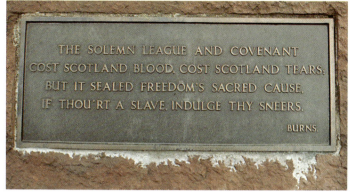

The pony does not mind that its rider wears the rosettes. If those ears were laid back, the signal could mean that Douglas Corrance should be thinking of a fine equine profile with the rosettes on the cheek strap.

Burns' solemn words in Biggar's tribute to its past are as double-edged as any blade that shed blood in those illiberal years, when religious zeal made sneering the least of the impositions of men upon one another.

Commercial glasshouses were
introduced into the Clyde Valley in
the 1930s after about sixty years of
the successful harvesting of fruit in
the summer. The controlled
environment, fuelled first by coal
and now by oil, allowed the growers
to produce crops all year round.
This is now a necessity to meet the
fuel bills and the competition from
Holland, where the growers' fuel
costs are subsidized. The main crop
is tomatoes. Sixteen-foot-long
plants are supported on those long
angled bars. Other crops include
lettuce and cucumber, sweet peas,
gladioli and chrysanthemums, and
even roses, orchids, carnations,
cacti, or, as here, begonias.

Craignethan Castle, a few miles from Lanark, was a stronghold of the Hamiltons from the fifteenth century until 1665. In the religious wars which plagued the reign of Mary, Queen of Scots, the Hamiltons supported Mary, who lost, so the Hamiltons lost the roof over their heads when the Protestant party partially dismantled it. The rectangular tower has an unusual ornate design and is the oldest part of the castle.

The building starred in another set of religious wars, albeit under an alias, for the Castle of Tillietudlem, the setting for much Covenanting incident in *Old Mortality,* was based by Sir Walter Scott on Craignethan.

'Now look, love,' says Dad, 'you don't put these great big juicy ones in your mouth, like this.'

'But, Daddy, that's the umpteenth time you've told me that. I'm the only one putting them in the basket.'

In 1872, two brothers, Robert and William Scott, decided to grow strawberries in the Clyde Valley. Whether they already knew that the Scots had what was to become a world-famous sweet tooth is not recorded, but Robert and William may just have helped to develop the Scottish taste for the sweet things in life. Soon after strawberries had proved to be a successful crop, R. & W. Scott combined them with sugar from the West Indies, imported through Greenock, to make the jam for the Scottish jeely pieces. Despite setbacks to the strawberry crop through red rot root disease, the 'berry has continued to grow successfully and has been joined by raspberries, gooseberries, and black and red currants. It may be that the terms of approval and disgust, 'the berries' and 'red rotten', are derived from the success and failure of the strawberry.

'There's gold in them thar hills!' The classic line brings to mind a picture of sunbaked mountains or perhaps that famous photograph of a long line of optimists struggling across a frozen Alaskan pass to reach the Klondike. Certainly, the last thing it would be likely to evoke would be the gently contoured Lowther Hills, although German and Dutch prospectors were searching for gold — and finding it — here as far back as the time of James IV. Gold from here was included in the Scottish crown, and we recall, not so very long ago, a local man who, if he liked your face, would pan enough gold to make you a wedding ring. The eponymous lead of Leadhills seems to have been a better commercial bet over the piece, the mines remaining productive until 1928.

The children hooping it up are not, however, embryonic forty-niners or Clementines of tomorrow. This octet is the entire primary school of Crawfordjohn in Lanarkshire. The obelisk is at Leadhills and commemorates William Symington, an engineering pioneer of steamships.

Controversy surrounds the true age of John Taylor, and there are sceptics who say that he lived only to the age of 134. He was working in the mines when he was a centenarian, and when it was suggested that the time had come for him to call it a day, he went off in an imperial huff, saying that had he known it was only a temporary job he would never have taken it on in the first place.

In his lifetime Taylor may have been present at the opening of the first lending library in the world, which was the gift to Leadhills from one of its native sons, Allan Ramsay. Ramsay, whose father was the superintendent of the mines, was born here in 1686 but left Leadhills in 1700. As far as we can make out, his contact with Leadhills thereafter was minimal, and one of his biographers explains it thus: 'We need only recall the exclusive character previously attributed to the people of Leadhills, their antipathy to any intrusion upon them by strangers of any kind, to understand the case. They were a type of Scottish Essenes, a close community, akin to the fisher-communities of Newhaven and Fisherrow, with their distinctive customs, traditions, and prejudices. . . .' In their lighter moments they were apparently addicted to quoiting, as the picture shows. And any group that has the 'kites' as its most popular pastime could not have been wholly bad.

He was a tiny little man with a disproportionate ego. As a poet, Allan Ramsay regarded Shakespeare and Homer as equals but did not hold this against them. He was hard-working, humorous, sociable, amiable, and uxorious. He deserves a place in such Scottish theatrical history as there is because of what he did and, more importantly, because of what he tried to do. What that was may be guessed from the Epilogue that he wrote for some forgotten drama, not necessarily his own and not necessarily Scottish:

'Shall London have its houses twa,
And we be doomed to nane awa?
Is our metropolis ance the place
Where lang-syne dwelt the royal race
Of Fergus, this gait dwindled doun
To the level o' a clachan toun?
While thus she suffers the desertion
O' a maist rational diversion.'

It was to remedy this situation that he built 'at vast expense' a playhouse in Carrubber's Close in Edinburgh. This enterprise was sabotaged by the inevitable clerical opposition, which made full use of an extraordinary statute of George II, which effectively banned theatre in any other city than London. London is still behaving as though that statute were in force.

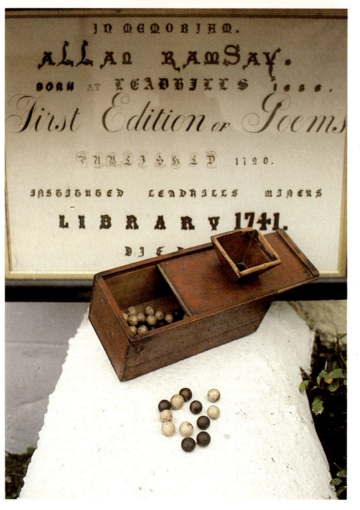

Nowadays, we tend to question, perhaps correctly, the deeds of charity of which our ancestors were so fond. Perhaps Freud has made us somewhat chary of accepting the surface explanation at the expense of the deeper, more authentic motivation. We have always regarded charity as one of the chillier virtues and one peculiarly prone to manipulation by hypocrisy. Also, it seems to be based on a kind of book-entry morality. Does the Nobel Prize justify nitroglycerine or even excuse it? Does Carnegie's largesse towards Dunfermline somehow wipe out his treatment of the steelworkers in America? Like Jesting Pilate, we do not wait for an answer, content to have indicated our scepticism with the question.

Allan Ramsay's gift to his native Leadhills in 1741 of what is claimed to have been the first circulating library in Britain raises similar doubts. Ramsay left Leadhills for Edinburgh at the age of fourteen, and it would appear that his gift of the library was his only contact with Leadhills thereafter. Was this Ramsay's roundabout way of saying that the people of the village in which he had been born were a bunch of illiterate, uneducated savages? And what are we to make of the box with his black and white balls for blackballing each other?

The story is told of the Buchanites, that weird religious sect founded by the strange Elspeth Buchan in the eighteenth century. Driven from Irvine, the Buchanites set off, like the ancient Israelites, in search of a Promised Land, and, passing through Ayrshire, they encountered an old man, digging. When urged to join them and to labour for the Lord in His garden, the old man refused, for the canny, Biblical reason that the Good Lord had a poor record as an employer, as witness his treatment of his last gardener, Adam.

Ian Hamilton Finlay, obviously, had no such qualms. We first made his acquaintance, many years ago, when he was a wunderkind at the Glasgow School of Art. Then successively he became a writer and a concrete poet. Now, in his garden at Dunsyre at the foot of the Pentland Hills he has merged all these talents to create something that is at once quirky and unique, in which the organic and inorganic compliment and complement each other beautifully.

The place is Cumnock, but it could be any other Ayrshire town on the evening of a wet day: the same expiring watery sunshine vainly defying the mercury-coloured tones of the approaching night. Everything, human or machine, grows towards its own silhouette, and the real street wavers and shrinks to the cosy dimensions of Coronation Street on the box.

Occasionally in our admittedly desultory reading of history we find ourself impatient with those historians who pride themselves on keeping an open mind. As well boast that you have a hole in your pocket, we think. Some historians seem to agonize perpetually about the Covenanters. Were they a bunch of religious fanatics or a genuine revolutionary movement? We see the Covenanters, Robert Burns, and Keir Hardie (founder of the Independent Labour Party whose bust, by Benno Schotz, stands outside Cumnock Town Hall) as part of the same thing.

The way some folks tell it, the Bachelors Club at Tarbolton was a kind of Ayrshire version of the notorious Hellfire Club. The burning truth is that it was an association of young men who met for 'mutual improvement and bodily regalement', and on it Robert Burns squandered three pence per month.

If there had been no Mauchline then Robert Burns would have had to invent one. And sometimes it seems that that is exactly what happened. Seldom can there have been such a close affinity between a poet's work and a specific place. From a productive point of view, Alloway and Mount Oliphant hardly even gave a hint of what was to come, but with the move to Mossgiel, the farm just a mile outside Mauchline, some magnificent spring was tapped. The winter of 1785—86 produced one masterpiece after another: 'The Twa Dogs', 'Address to the Deil', 'The Vision', 'Halloween', 'To a Mouse', 'The Cotter's Saturday Night', 'The Ordination', and 'The Jolly Beggars', which both Thomas Carlyle and Matthew Arnold judged to be his finest work and which is indelibly associated with Poosie Nansie's tavern.

Nowadays, when Scotland seems to be filled with tourists clicking Japanese cameras, we may find it difficult to believe that foreigners of an earlier day were less than enthralled by the country. As far back as 1617, Sir Anthony Weldon was quoted as saying that if Judas had betrayed his Lord in Scotland he 'had scarce got a tree to hang himself'. Sir William Brereton rode a hundred miles without seeing any timber, and two centuries earlier Pope Pius II described Scotland as destitute of trees. Dr Samuel Johnson, more picturesquely, said that a tree in Scotland was as rare as a horse in Venice. Henry Grey Graham declares that at the start of the eighteenth century throughout Ayrshire 'the country was one huge naked waste; not a tree was to be seen in the open land, and none to be found anywhere except by the banks of the Doon, the Girvan, and the Stinchar, whereon little knots of stunted oaks and beeches took shelter'. Is it too much to listen to the flat Ayrshire voice and to hear in it the vocal reflection of the flat featureless landscape described by Henry Grey Graham?

The Ayrshire of today makes belated amends to all these critical, tree-starved travellers. The bottom picture on the left shows that there are trees just outside Kilmarnock while the two immediately above it show the vicinity of Dalmellington. Dalmellington is where the hills begin and the lonely hill farms and the curlews. In the centre of the town there is an ancient fort-hill which attests to the continuity of this little town where the inhabitants have been weavers, miners, and now have come full circle back to textiles.

There is a vast difference between saying that your home is your castle and declaring that your castle is your home. The first statement has vaguely threatening overtones of unwelcoming men on the battlements with vats of boiling oil; the second has a cosy domesticity. The Victorians understood this, which is probably why there is an element of pastiche in their building. Their castles look backwards to Abbotsford and Sir Walter Scott. When they look forward they seem to be anticipating Hollywood. Their castles have gardens in which palm trees grow alongside snapdragons and where there always seems to be a faint if anachronistic echo of Percy Grainger's music:

Who ever saw
A hairy great outlaw,
In a Scottish country garden?

These castles look across gentle hills where no men at arms lurk with deadly intent. Their sheep and cattle graze peacefully and safely. The bottom picture shows Penkill Castle, near Girvan, which is worthy of special mention, if only because our photographer, Douglas Corrance, fell madly in love with it, which only goes to prove that even the most skilled of photographers can sometimes get his dreams in soft focus.

Hull down, or maybe hull up, on the horizon the rock rears itself 1114 feet out of the sea. Experts describe it as a syenitic greenstone, and who are we to say them nay. We used to stare at it across the Firth of Clyde and wonder who christened it with the name of an Annie S. Swan heroine. To us it was always Paddy's Milestone, which indicates where most of us came from, but more refined people referred to it as Ailsa Craig. We knew that it was famous for curling stones and lonely students counting gannets.

Murray's *Handbook for Scotland (1894)* is rather snooty about Girvan, which it describes as a dull but neat town at the mouth of the Girvan Water, consisting of one long street. Girvan's comments on Murray are not recorded.

There's the church
And there's the steeple;
Thoosans o' gulls
But gey few people.
Ah gave up the coont
Et a million an' one,
When the seabirds stertit
Tae darken the sun,
And Ah heard them mew
An' better mew
'Panic, grass
An' feverfew'.
An' high o'er Girvan
The rainbow sign:
Nae mair watter,
The fire nixt time.

Turnberry (for the benefit of those upwardly mobile who like to drop the occasional name) was once the seat of the Earls of Carrick, and in its castle, now a ruin, Robert Bruce was probably born. Those who for various reasons prefer to drop names in a different region will opt for Lochmaben in Dumfriesshire as Bruce's birthplace. Either way it no longer matters, being in the past, which, as every schoolboy knows, is strictly for psychiatrists. Today, the swords and battle-axes have been beaten into putters and number-three irons, and Turnberry is famous for its two championship golf courses and its extremely upmarket hotel, where Bruce would probably be turned away for not wearing a tie.

Pictured below is ruined Dunure Castle, where the fourth Earl of Cassillis roasted the Abbot of Crossraguel on a gridiron.

We hear a great deal about guilt by association but not quite so much about immortality by the same means. Yet who would remember Beatrice but for Dante? Or Ethel le Neve without Hawley Harvey Crippen? Or Clara Petacci minus Mussolini? Or Lord Alfred Douglas away from Oscar Wilde? The list is endless and only proves, if it proves anything, what the ancient Greeks already knew, that immortals have the power to bestow their own immortality, in whole or in part, on lesser mortals.

There is a kind of secondary immortality which must be hard to bear, granted that we are allowed such ordinary human feelings as vanity in the afterlife. This immortality might be described as immortality of the alter ego and is perhaps diminished because of that. Yet an alter ego is better than no ego at all, and there is always the reassuring possibility that some mad scholar will excavate the truth and restore the ego to its rightful, undisguised integrity.

What has Douglas Graham done that the ages should cherish him? He lived and died in his small village, the happiest of nonentities. No comet blazed across the sky to announce his birth, no star wept blood on his passing. The same might be said about John Davidson, who should not be confused with the unfortunate Victorian poet of the same name. Our John Davidson was a village cobbler, or soutar, in Kirkoswald. Now Soutar Johnnie sits in the garden of his Kirkoswald cottage with Douglas Graham, a.k.a. Tam O'Shanter, both of them perhaps more stoned than usual but still obviously the darlings of contemporary Ayrshire men. The real cronies are buried in Kirkoswald cemetery.

Culzean Castle is a piece of pure theatre. Built on the top of a cliff overlooking the Firth of Clyde, it tries hard but unsuccessfully to pretend that it is real Gothic, but no one takes the attempt seriously. The great architect, Robert Adam, probably set out in 1771 with the best of macabre intentions, but he failed to foresee a generation that could take films about chainsaw massacres in its stride. The menace of the sinister, convoluted tree in Culzean Country Park is perhaps more to its taste. At midnight it changes into a homicidal druid with a golden sickle.

The statue of Robert Burns in Ayr has an enigmatic quality. To begin with, the Bard has his back turned to the town and his expression seems to indicate, as indeed do his folded arms and general attitude, that he is in an imperial huff. Possibly he is miffed at the sculptor or whoever was responsible for setting him where he could not see what was happening in the town which he praised for its honest men and bonnie lassies. Or have his aesthetic susceptibilities been disturbed by the red roses in the garden behind the Alloway cottage in which he was born? Certainly, we do not remember them when we last visited Burns' Cottage, which was before rose growers grew rich and affected muttonchop whiskers.

As a county town, Ayr has seen them all: the Burns's, the Bruces and the Wallaces, the famous and the infamous, the good, the bad, and the in betweens. Our personal gold star, however, goes to a most unlikely candidate, a hangman. His name was William Sutherland, and he was a Highlander. After the Pentland Rising in 1666, eight of the prisoners were condemned to death at Ayr. The local executioner showed his sympathy with the doomed Covenanters by disappearing, whereupon Sutherland, the Irvine hangman, was brought by force to Ayr to carry out the grisly job. This he refused to do. He was threatened with torture, to no avail. Eventually, he was bound to a stake and a cap was drawn over his head. Four soldiers loaded their matchlocks and lit their matches. Sutherland remained firm, and finally the provost offered life and a free pardon to any prisoner who would hang the others. The offer was accepted by one Cornelius Anderson, who, after begging their forgiveness, hanged his seven comrades, thus enabling the official face to be saved. Sutherland was thrown into prison, where he remained for several weeks before being released into limbo.

The top picture shows Newmarket Street with its Regency and Georgian echoes, while the bottom picture shows the only pub in Ayr that closes at 8.30 p.m. on a Saturday night, the landlady declaring that her weekend is as sacrosanct as her customers'. This suggests to us that in a circuitous and attenuated way the spirit of William Sutherland is not dead.

We have always regarded Kilmarnock as a down-to-earth, rather pragmatic town. Bonnets, boots, and carpets was the triad that we lesser mortals who lived farther down the Ayrshire coast believed in, long after the Kilmarnock bonnet had joined the bustle in whatever sartorial limbo awaits the out of date. We might, if pressed, have added whisky, even if only to honour Johnnie Walker, the grocer in King Street who, in 1820, invented the hangover and all that goes with it. Most of all, however, we held Kilmarnock in high respect because of a small printer called John Wilson. In an era when the Select Society in Edinburgh changed its name to the Society for Promoting the Reading and Speaking of the English Language and when even David Hume paid good hard cash to quasi-missionaries from the south who claimed to eradicate the dour provincialism of the Doric from his speech, the aforementioned John Wilson undertook to publish the poems of Robert Burns and brought out the famous Kilmarnock Edition. Burns saw the Edition through the press while he was hiding in the town from the legal beagles who had been set on him by Jean Armour's father.

The local shop window suggests that this sturdy independence still survives, even to the idiosyncratic spelling of 'peasemeal'. The continued survival of peasemeal indicates a staunch disregard for come-and-go dietary fashions.

The tombstones commemorate the Killing Time of the seventeenth century, when every Covenanter was potentially his own war memorial.

A walk along Fenwick Water will bring you to Dean Castle, once the fort of the Boyds, who were Earls of Kilmarnock. These days there is no point in leaving your calling card, the last earl having been beheaded in 1746 and being consequently now unable to read it. The top pair of pictures show the castle, but the real subject of the photographs is early autumn which seems able to upstage everything chromatically. The bright red hips in the foreground of one of the pictures are patiently waiting to be turned into vitamin C by some enthusiastic amateur herbalist. There is nothing sacred to the encroaching autumn, which even manages to turn Afton Water, apostrophized by Robert Burns, into a green and gold song of praise to itself.

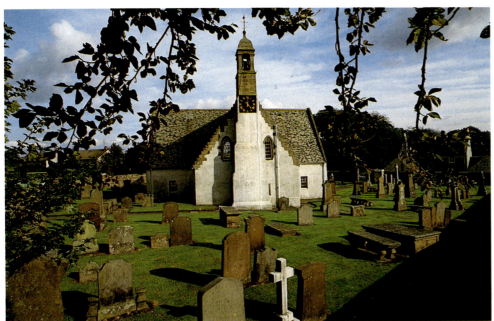

Fenwick is Covenanterland. The delightful little church, which has been restored, was built originally in 1643 and contains a pre-Reformation pulpit. You may still see, and even try on for size, the 'jougs' which the minister is seen shaking at you rather unconvincingly. Previous incumbents would have fastened them round your neck and left you as a malefactor to be jeered at by the congregation. The hourglass suggests that you might have preferred the jougs to the boredom of 'three mile prayers and half-mile graces'.

Irvine has every reason to be proud of its associations with Robert Burns and John Galt, who is, to our way of thinking, a *truer* Scottish novelist than Sir Walter Scott. Both Burns and Galt were realists, telling it the way it was, whereas the Great Unknown always seems to be telling it as it should have been, from the viewpoint of a romantic Scottish High Tory. This may be just another way of expressing the eternal rivalry between east and

west, or it may be a different way of pointing out different social origins. Burns and Galt, who was born in Irvine in 1779, were essentially men of their time, and Galt's book *The Provost* is almost a prose equivalent of 'Holy Willie's Prayer'. Burns' stay in the town was short and ended when a relative's house was burned down. He had been training to become a flax dresser, or 'heckler', something we thought he had been all his life.

Last night we dreamed we were at Manderley again, only it turned out to be just like Brodick Castle in Arran. We are talking about the inside of the Castle of course, the part that you plebians never see. Anyway, there was the same candelabra from which dear Max used to swing during his frequent and unpredictable bouts of rage when someone mentioned Rebecca. The same ornate ceiling was there; how I remember the number of times I lay staring up at it after dear Max had knocked me down. Everything was curiously still as I wandered round, expecting at any moment to see the evil features of that sinister housekeeper in one of the mirrors. Did I ever live here, I asked myself wonderingly as I went slowly round the elegant room, recalling the old masters and remembering the old mistress. Somehow she seemed to be everywhere, as though she was waiting patiently for the woman from *The House Beautiful* or the man from Sotheby's. Then I was aware of a light footfall and was conscious of a faint scent of *muguet de bois.* The door began to open slowly, and I looked towards it, waiting and dreading what I might see. Then suddenly I was outside a small white cottage in Corrie, and someone was saying 'You just missed the Princess of Wales, Jimmy. Will I bring in your red carpet?'

The disconsolate gentleman with the shipped oars sits just offshore of Largs, like a Viking who slept in and missed the Battle of Largs. Around him, the spinnakers flare as the small yachts buzz about like dragonflies. In the far distance the peaks of Arran show appropriately the Sleeping Warrior, and between him and them lies the Great Cumbrae where once a local minister invoked a blessing on his little island and the adjacent islands of Great Britain and Ireland.

If the depressed gentleman is the Viking we imagine, then his depression is understandable. We ourself would hardly be overjoyed at the prospect of explaining our not turning up to an angry king who had just lost a battle and with it the Hebrides and the Isle of Man. In the circumstances, we would

have declared ourself an exile and sought consolation in Nardini's, which seems to have been around long enough to be contemporaneous with a famous and historically crucial thirteenth-century battle. Actually it dates back to the Thirties, and we would not be surprised if some kind of move were not afoot to have it declared a listed building. We read somewhere recently an article in which Nardini's was discussed approvingly as an example of Thirties architecture, when architects seemed to think that cinemas and cafes must be made to resemble luxury cruise liners. We ourself tasted our first sundae in Nardini's. Until then we were under the impression that Sunday was the dullest day of the week and that the people of Largs could not spell.

The coat of arms of Paisley is too old a device to reflect the source of the town's world renown. When the proud members of the corporation of the largest town in Scotland raised this emblem, they could not know and would never have believed that their well-rounded solid-sounding title would, in leaner, meaner times, disappear altogether.

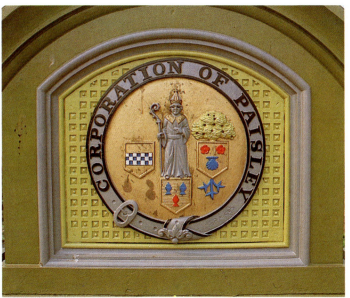

Paisley's prosperity and the fortunes of the Clark and Coats families are reflected in the Italianate town hall which seems to front the square but is flanked by the White Cart Water. Paisley had two sources of water power for its early textile industry: the White Cart Water and the Black Cart Water. Pollution from the industrial mills made the White black and the Black white.

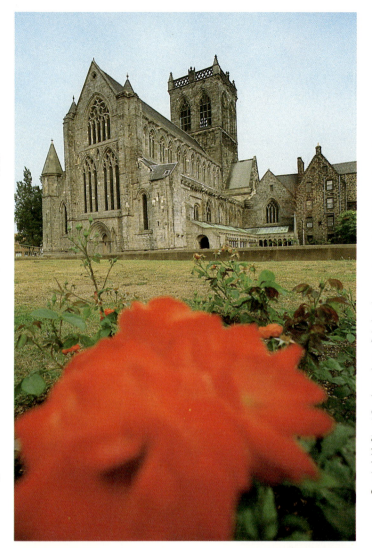

The Abbey of Paisley was founded in 1163 by Benedictine monks. It was one of a number of abbeys set up in Scotland as part of the religious reforms introduced by Saint Margaret who first invited the Benedictines to Dunfermline. Other Scottish abbeys of this period include Dryburgh and Melrose, Newbattle and Holyrood. This is not the original abbey church. The English destroyed that building in 1307 during their ferocious invasion and occupation of Scotland under Edward I. This period saw the rise and fall of such local heroes and villains as William Wallace, Robert Bruce, and John Balliol. This particular abbey church was built in the middle of the fifteenth century and contains the bodies of Robert III, who died in 1406 after a reign of remarkable incompetence, and Princess Marjory, daughter of Robert Bruce and founder of the Stewart royal line. There is also a chapel of Saint Mirin, the patron saint of Paisley, better known as Saint Mirren and as a football team. The building was extensively restored at the beginning of this century and is used as the Parish Church of Paisley.

The certainty of religious belief, which once inspired the people of early Paisley to contribute their work and wealth to help the monks build the Abbey Church, gave way in time to a more enquiring frame of mind. This sought to discover the meaning of life in the hall of the Paisley Philosophical Institution and to study the limits of the universe at the Coats Observatory. It may not be idle to imagine that glass plates which had been exposed at the Observatory to catch the light of and record the position of the stars and planets would have been developed and studied in the Photographic Rooms of the Philosophical Institution. The Paisley buddies who helped build the Abbey Church had little time to contemplate the universe, but the monks would have told them that their world was the centre of it. Their descendants, who built the Philosophical Institution and the Coats Observatory, knew for certain that the world was not the centre of the universe, but they believed that Britain was the centre of the world.

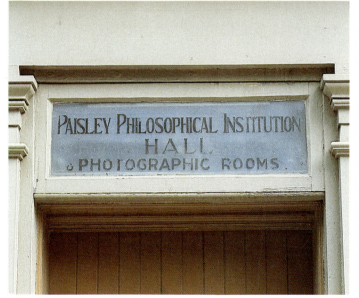

The balanced ascent and descent of these staircases within the elegant proportions of Paisley's Museum and Art Gallery is reminiscent of a famous puzzle in perception in which a staircase built around the walls of a large hall continues in an unbroken sequence of ascent and descent. This reminder of deceiving appearances may lead us to see not Paisley's world-famous pattern, but the face of a Muppet-like monster with a touch of the grotesque: its eyes contain two beetles. Even the Paisley wally tile is not all it appears to be. Behind the gentle appearance of a tulip lie the malevolent eye and ferocious tusks of a wild boar.

Wally closes themselves were often deceiving. Once through the close and on to the stairs, the tiles gave way to mere painted plasterwork. Paisley would have had its share of such closes, as well as those in which the art of the tile maker was allied to the craft of the tile layer as the precisely parallel lines swept us up all ten flights of stairs to the fifth floor. However, did craft and art ever come together in Paisley to decorate that mythical feature of the better-off back court — the wally midden?

Look again at the Paisley pattern, for, according to one expert, deception of a kind is indeed involved here. That famous Scottish leaf is actually a date palm leaf, adopted by the Babylonians a long time ago as a symbol of life. With the export of civilization to India, the symbol travelled to India and eventually to Kashmir, where it was incorporated into shawls. Came the Raj, and the symbol and the shawl travelled to England, from there to Edinburgh, and, last of all, in the early eighteen hundreds to Paisley which promptly appropriated them. The town certainly drew life from the pattern for a while, but eventually had its comeuppance when fashion took a hand. The properly dressed lady of the 1870s was loath to hide her bustle under a shawl, and it and its industry quickly dropped from the fashion scene.

Paisley weavers were a rare breed. The only sport they would have anything to do with was curling, otherwise they were real Arts and Craft men with a penchant for poetry. Robert Tannahill was an early weaver-poet, but another whose fame was greater, if not his poetry, was William McGonagall.

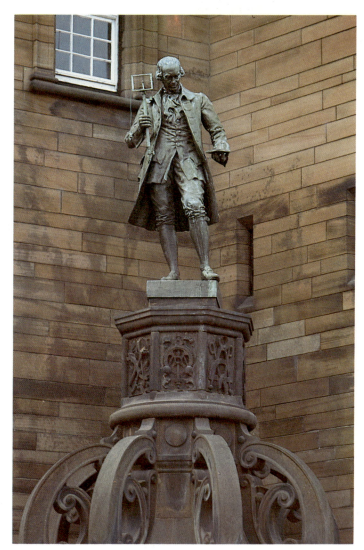

This famous son of Greenock is contemplating an ancient problem. Not, however, the problem which he solved to found his own fortune and contribute to Britain's prosperity and to the eventual display of civic pride which is embodied in Greenock's Italianate spire, the classical facade alongside, and the audacity of Victorian craftsmen who wrought iron to look like lace. Mr James Watt's problem is as old as life on earth — how does the little fly know when to fly away?

Greenock's prosperity was based on the coming and going of ships. Its occasional decline was due to the coming and going of the need for ships. James Watt contributed to the early prosperity of his home town by working on the improvement of the harbour and the deepening of the Clyde. During its long history as the first port on the Clyde, Greenock has seen thousands of ships and millions of men come and go, and waited in vain for some of them to return. Hence the blessing offered by the citizens of Greenock to sailors who refreshed themselves with a drink of water at the sign of the blue lion.

In the days when the blue lion first offered both blessing and refreshment, the men who left Greenock in ships were all sailors. Nowadays, those men whose place of work is the sea are more accurately called seamen. Sailors are those people in blue plimsolls and thick white sweaters and funny little woollen bonnets who go to sea for fun and adventure, and who in tall ships seek the challenges which earlier sailors had forced upon them by wind and sea and the demands of shipowners and merchants.

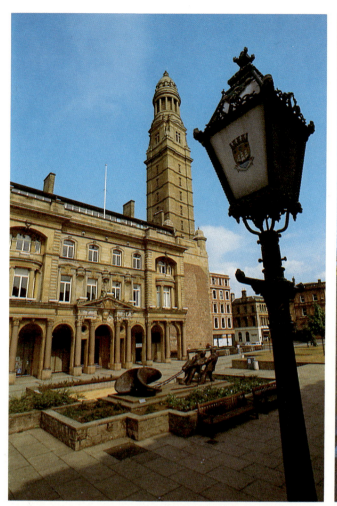

While the old men forever pull that propeller screw down the shipyard of the past, the young men of Greenock must hope that oil demand makes further exploitation of the British seas a worthwhile plan for money, so that oil platforms may rise, however ungainly, on the Clyde.

Whatever the past promised, or the present offers, the future has no fears for four old friends. Mrs Paisley has just delivered a punch line which, ever so slightly shocking, was nonetheless hilarious. 'But wait,' she says, 'you've not heard the worst of it.' The fourth friend has.

There is nothing odd about the National Dock Labour Board sharing premises with the Sugar Association. Dock workers and importers always shared, albeit unequally, in the prosperity which came to Greenock with the cane sugar from the West Indies. Nowadays, both share the lack of prosperity, and a cold harsh wind blows through Greenock's docks.

Before the shipyards of Greenock built steam ships, they built sailing ships. Then, the riverside was overlooked by ship's masts, and the sound of the river was of ropes, sheets, halyards and ratlines clattering and rattling in the breeze. Now the riverbank is overlooked by giant cranes but too often the sound of the river is silence. For one weekend in 1984 the riverside was once again overlooked by masts and by fearless young sailors with sea legs any old Greenock sailor would have been proud of.

When an old ship acquires a new owner, it frequently acquires a new name. One man's *Bellerophon* is another man's *Nemesis*. We may not know any of the names of the three-master, but we may safely assume none was as self-deprecating as that of the yacht. We could always guess: *Pride of Strathclyde* (but she flies the wrong cross), *Pride of Erin?* What do you think?